THE BEADING OF MY HEART

52 LOOM BEADING PROJECTS
INTRODUCING THE MINI-FRAME LOOM

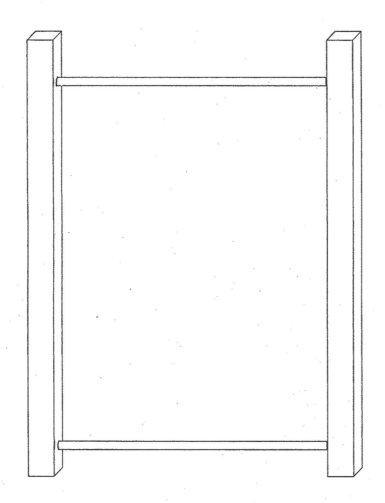

HUAUTE BEADWEAVER
MARY L. THOMPSON

Eagle's View Publishing
A WestWind, Inc. Company
6756 North Fork Road
Liberty, UT 84310

Library of Congress Number: 99-096739
ISBN 0-943604-60-5

First Edition

with respect for
beloved teachers

Genny Mitchell

and

June LeGrand

10 9 8 7 6 5 4 3 2 1

CONTENTS

TEXT ILLUSTRATIONS

PATTERN PICTURES

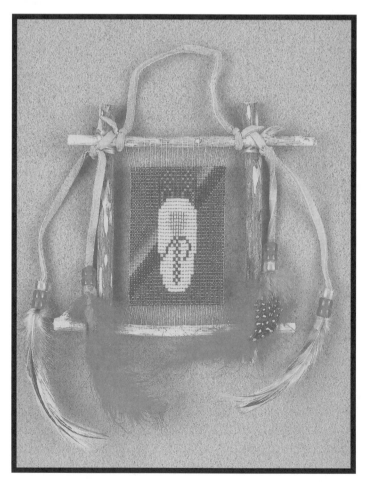

Cradleboard Suncatcher or Hanging Decoration

1. Description Of The Mini-Frame Loom

The mini-frame loom is based on the looms used by early peoples for fabric, blanket and rug weaving, as well as for beadweaving.

The early frame looms were constructed of sticks, and designed to accommodate the desired size of the finished project. These looms could be easily stored for future projects, or could be taken apart and returned to nature. When the life-style was nomadic, it must have been a pleasure to have one less item to pack up and move.

The frame loom can be used for two different styles of weaving: single surface or continuous warp. The continuous warp style requires a slightly different warping technique. A larger frame loom than addressed here is also recommended.

The single surface style of beadweaving is the technique used and described in this book. The crafter will not only be able to complete a mini-frame project, but will also learn the basics of loom beading. These basics can be carried over to the use of larger frame looms, as well as the other types of beading looms available today.

The mini-frame loom is designed specifically for single surface beadweaving. The work can be left on the loom, turning the mini-frame loom into a miniature frame for the loomed picture. This framed picture can be used as a suncatcher, or other decorative ornament. It can also be mounted on a base. By constructing a slightly larger mini-frame loom, it will be possible to remove the finished work from the loom. These loomed strips can be stitched onto garments or accessories (such as barrettes or bags/pouches). The section on "Other Ideas" offers suggestions and will, hopefully, encourage the imagination to take flight.

1.1 Woman Using Frame Loom

2. Materials and Tools Needed

LOOM

The majority of the patterns in this book are designed to fit a mini-frame loom with a working area (center opening) measuring not less than 3 inches x 4 inches. Chapter 4 (Loom Preparation) covers the construction of three different styles of mini-frame looms. Please refer to this Chapter to determine the type of loom to be constructed, and the tools and materials required for construction. When working on a larger pattern, the loom working area must be adjusted accordingly. The patterns are marked with the size loom required. The patterns do not have to be worked on a mini-frame loom, but can be worked on any home-built or commercial beading loom.

PATTERNS

Use the patterns in this book, modify them, or create something personal, using standard beading grid paper (samples of which are included in the back of this book). The largest pattern recommended on the 3" x 4" mini-frame loom, using size 11° seed beads, is 45 rows long (horizontal rows) and 40 rows wide (vertical rows). By using smaller beads, a more detailed picture is possible. More horizontal and vertical rows will fit into the same work area. Grids have been supplied for the 3" x 4" mini-frame loom using size 10°, 11°, 12°, 13° and 14° Czech seed beads; 11° and 12° Czech 2-cuts; and Japanese "delica" beads.

BEADS

The patterns in this book are labeled with the bead size and type used. The size 11° Czech seed bead is used most often. The wide range of colors and styles (opaque, matte, transparent, aurora borealis or AB, etc.) combined with the ease of use (compared to smaller beads) makes the size 11° seed bead an excellent choice for this project. Size 11° Japanese seed beads can also be used.

The size 11° and 12° 2-cuts are more difficult to work with than the seed beads. The 2-cut bead is more square than round, and the ends are often uneven. Additionally, because of the different shape of the beads, care must be taken when designing the pattern. The end result is "sparkly" and beautiful, but more work is involved in choosing the most uniformly shaped beads. These beads are not recommended for the beginning beader.

The Japanese "delica" or "delicious" beads are very uniform in size. Some crafters compare them to size 12° seed beads. The delicas work beautifully in loomed beadwork. These beads are generally sold by the gram, in small plastic bags or tubes. They are comparatively more expensive than the standard seed beads, but since the mini-frame loom picture is a small project, it could be worth the additional expense, and deserves consideration.

A combination of transparent background and opaque central figure (as with the Kokopelli pattern) can be very dramatic. Be careful though when combining different types of beads. Be sure all the beads for the project are the same size. It is also recommended that the beginning beader not mix Czech and Japanese beads. The Japanese seed bead size 11° will be slightly larger and more square than the Czech seed bead. If care is not taken when choosing the beads, the end result could be very disappointing.

A mini-frame loom picture that will be hanging in a window, in direct sunlight, will need beads that won't easily fade. A simple way to test beads for colorfastness is to put some in a dish, or string a number of them on a thread. Place (or hang) the beads in direct sunlight for at least a week. Keep the rest of the beads in a container out of direct light. At the end of the week, compare the exposed beads to the others to determine the amount of fade (if any). Some of the bright pinks and purple hues tend to fade quickly, as well as some of the bright yellows. Avoid using beads that have been dyed.

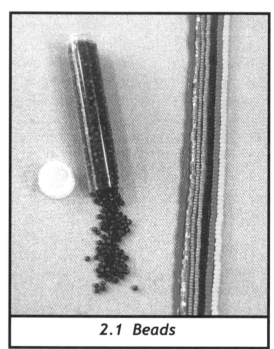

Seed beads come in various types of containers, as well as on hanks. Buying beads by the hank is preferred. When beads are in containers, it is difficult to get a good look at the color and size uniformity. A full hank of beads generally consists of 12 strands of beads, with all ends joined into a single knot. The number of beads per strand and number of beads per hank varies with the size of the bead (see TIPS). Remember, the higher the number, the smaller the bead. Always handle hanks of beads by carefully holding the knot.

2.1 Beads

THREAD

The WARP thread is the thread wrapped around the loom. This process is called "warping the loom". The WEFT thread is the actual working thread that will pass through the beads. It can be confusing remembering which is "warp" and which is "weft". One way to get them straight is:

After you
WRAP the WARP
what is
LEFT is WEFT

Beading thread used for loomwork is a nylon blend, specially made for this purpose. While silk and cotton blends are used for different beading techniques, they are not recommended for loom beading. They lack the necessary strength and durability. Use "Nymo" thread, or another similar nylon blend.

When beading a piece that will have to stand up to some stress, e.g., wristbands, belts, etc., the recommended warp thread is size "D". The recommended weft is a size "B". When the piece is to remain on the loom, it is possible to use finer threads. For these projects, use "B" Nymo for the warp, and "O" Nymo for the weft. For pieces that will later be sewn onto a bag, barrette or garment where minimal stress will occur, the "B" and "O" combination above will still work. If the piece is to be sewn onto a moccasin toe, for instance, it is better to use heavier threads if possible.

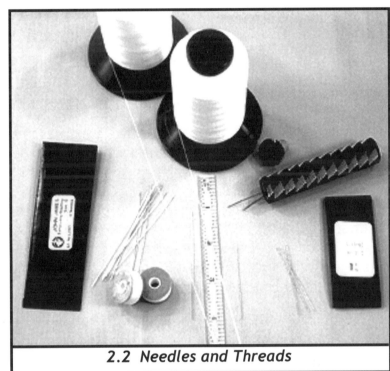

The smaller the beads used, the finer the thread will have to be. This will make it easier to pass the needle and thread through the beads 2, 3 or even 4 times as needed. <u>Remember</u> when working with transparent beads, colored threads will show through and can darken the piece, giving it a muddy appearance. Always use white thread with transparent beads. To strengthen a piece loomed with very small beads and fine thread, it is helpful to fill the beads with thread. In other words, start with a new length of thread, and pass through all the rows of the finished piece <u>at least</u> one more time.

2.2 Needles and Threads

NEEDLES

When working with size 11° transparent seed beads, or size 11° 2-cuts, a size #12XL (extra long) beading needle is recommended. This needle is flexible enough to work in the limited space available, and strong enough not to snap. The extra length makes it easier to pass back through all the beads of a wide row.

Some bead manufacturers make beads with smaller holes. If it becomes difficult to pass the needle back through the beads, it is better to switch to a finer needle than to try forcing the needle through. Forcing can cause weft thread to split and fray where it passes through the eye of the needle. There is also the added risk of breaking a bead or snapping the needle. Remove the larger needle, and replace it with a finer #13 needle.

When using beads smaller than size 11°, a finer needle than the above #12XL may be needed. A size #13 needle is recommended for beads sized 12° and 13°. Again, some manufacturers make beads with smaller holes. It may be necessary to use a #15 needle. Experiment with different size needles to find what will work best with the beads. The higher the number, the finer the needle will be.

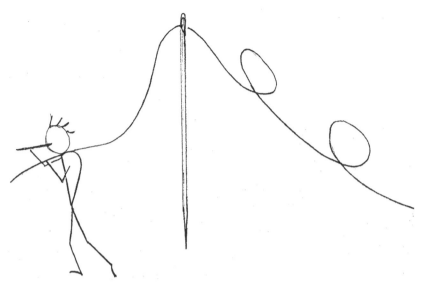

OTHER TOOLS NEEDED

* a small pair of sharp scissors (the size used for embroidery are best)
* a small pair of jewelers-size flat nose pliers can be used to aid in gripping the needle
* a magnifying glass, or a pair of magnifying glasses for those who would like the extra help
* a small scoop or teaspoon, for scooping up spilled beads
* glue for securing warp knots (any all-purpose, clear-drying glue will work, e.g., Fray Check™ which is available where sewing notions are sold)
* bee's wax is optional for weft threads, to help prevent knotting, tangling and fraying.
* see Chapter 4 (Loom Preparation) for additional materials and tools required for construction and preparation of the mini-frame loom

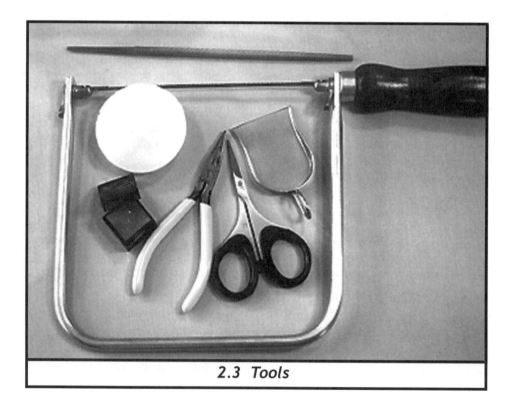

2.3 Tools

3. SETTING UP A WORK AREA

A good work area includes:

A. Enough space to lay the pattern down where it can be easily seen and followed.

B. A safe place to set out the beads. There are many different techniques for setting out beads; each person has his or her own preferences. Following are just a few examples:

1. a small amount of each color bead to be used is placed in one bowl, to be picked through as needed.

2. beads are separated by color into individual bowls, trays or other containers.

3. small piles of each color bead to be used are placed on a piece of fabric or scrap leather.

4. one thread is loosened from each hank of beads, and the beads are taken directly from that thread as needed.

The technique used for setting out the beads is determined by space availability and permanence. If a TV tray in a quiet corner is the best place to be found, then set up the work area accordingly.

C. Don't forget the importance of proper lighting. Sunlight is warm and wonderful, but the glare of strong sunlight off white pattern paper or book pages can, for many people, cause painful headaches and eye strain. Insufficient lighting can also lead to similar problems. Use good judgment.

An adjustable overhead light source, with a 60 Watt soft white bulb works well indoors. Others have recommended the use of a fluorescent style light. There are a few styles of fluorescent available equipped with a magnifying glass in the center.

When working for any length of time under artificial overhead light, consider investing in a smaller desk type light, to send light into the work area from a different angle. This will help eliminate the problem of working in the shadow of ones own hands.

D. Set out tools and other supplies where they can be easily reached when needed. If a permanent work area is not available, use a small box or basket to keep all working materials and tools together.

3.1 Work Table

8

4. Loom Preparation

The mini-frame loom, as needed for the patterns shown in this book, can be constructed in different ways. Three of these are included here. One can be accomplished by finding small sticks under or near a favorite tree. The other two require purchasing materials from the local lumber or craft store. The following directions are to be used as guidelines for actual construction. If a pattern has been chosen which will be removed from the loom after completion, then the length and/or width of the loom center opening will need adjustment. Check the pattern guidelines to determine the loom size required. NOTE: Do Not use Balsa wood for any of these mini-frame looms. It is too soft.

GATHERING MATERIALS AND CONSTRUCTION

MATERIALS:
> 2 - 5" x 1/4" diameter sticks
> 2 - 4" x 1/4" diameter sticks
> 2 to 3 yards imitation sinew or scrap leather strips/lacing
> wood glue or white all-purpose glue

TOOLS:
> pencil or awl
> hack saw or coping saw
> small round wood rasp
> fine grit sandpaper (120 grit or similar)

Finding small sticks (also referred to as "gathering") can be a very rewarding way to begin a project. Not only is it a good excuse to be outdoors, getting some exercise, but there is also the added satisfaction of "creating" something from the ground up (no pun intended).

The materials needed are small, sturdy sticks, not less than 1/4" thick. Please do not pull branches off of the trees. There are always pieces on the ground that can be used. The mini-frame loom will need four dry sticks: two (2) cut to 4" long, and two (2) cut to 5" long. The two shorter sticks must be smooth to prevent the thread from fraying and weakening. Sand the pieces with fine grit sandpaper (120 grit or similar). After sanding off the rough spots, the wood can be painted or stained, or it can be left natural. Be sure all pieces are completely dry prior to assembly.

To assemble the loom, lay the two longer sticks vertically on a flat surface. The two shorter sticks are then placed horizontally across the two longer ones, as shown in Diagram 4.1. Adjust the sticks to leave a rectangular opening of not less than 3" x 4". With a pencil or awl, mark each vertical

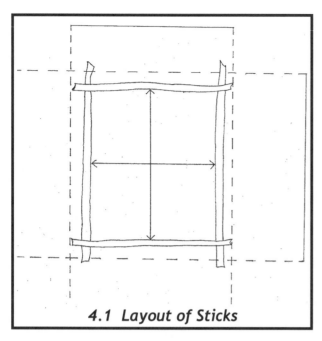

4.1 Layout of Sticks

(side) stick where it is overlapped by the horizontal stick. Using a small round or half-round wood rasp, lightly file the marked area until a shallow indentation appears as shown in Diagram 4.2. This small indentation will help prevent the top and bottom sticks from shifting out of position.

Place a small dot of glue (wood or all-purpose) into each indentation, and then lay the top and bottom sticks in place. Double check opening measurements, then allow glue to dry before continuing.

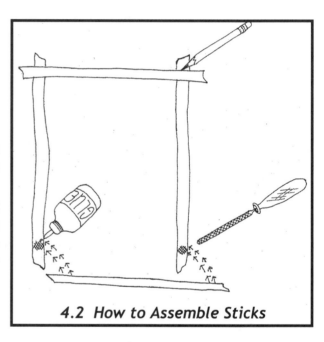

4.2 How to Assemble Sticks

Using imitation sinew or dampened leather lacing, make an "X" lashing at each corner (see Diagram 4.3). Secure the lashing with a square knot. It is best to have all knots on the same side of the loom. The ends can be trimmed close to the knot, or left long and used to add an accent feather or fetish (refer to Chapter 6: Finishing Touches). Allow the glue and dampened leather to dry thoroughly prior to warping the loom.

If purchasing materials from the lumber or craft store will work out better, here are two different styles, with the easier of the two listed first.

PURCHASING MATERIALS AND CONSTRUCTION

MATERIALS - TYPE 1:
    18" of 3/16" to 1/4" diameter dowel
        cut into: 2 - 5" length
                2 - 4" lengths
    wood glue or all-purpose glue
    2 to 3 yards imitation sinew
        or scrap leather strips/lacing
    paint or stain as desired

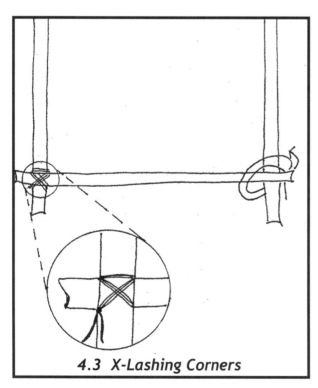

4.3 X-Lashing Corners

TOOLS:
        pencil or awl
        hack saw or coping saw
        small round or half-round wood rasp
        fine grit sandpaper (120 grit or similar)

This first style of mini-frame loom using purchased materials is quite simple, and requires fewer tools and less "tool-handling" expertise. It is made completely of dowel rod, available in craft, lumber and hardware stores in a variety of sizes and lengths.

Purchase a length of dowel rod, with a diameter not smaller than 3/16" nor larger than 1/4". Dowel rod comes in 3 foot and 4 foot lengths, and will have to be cut to size. Approximately 18" is needed for each mini-frame loom. Using a fine-toothed coping saw or a hack saw, cut two (2) pieces 5" long each. These will be the two side (vertical) pieces. Cut two (2) pieces 4" long each. These will be the top and bottom pieces (horizontal; see Diagram 4.4). Assemble this loom in the same manner as the one made of gathered sticks (please refer to Diagrams 4.2 and 4.3).

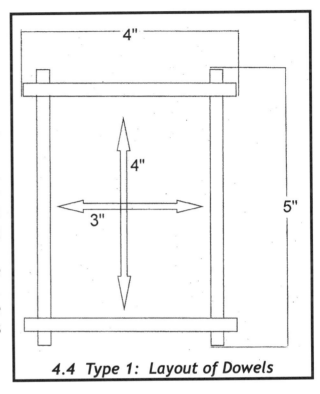

4.4 Type 1: Layout of Dowels

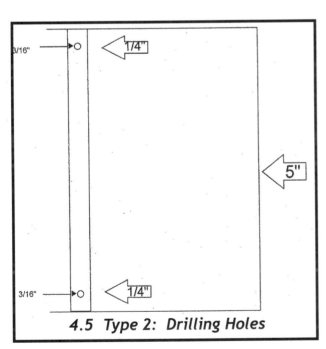

4.5 Type 2: Drilling Holes

MATERIALS - TYPE 2:
    6-1/2" of 3/16" diameter dowel (cut into 2 equal pieces)
    10" of 1/4" square pine (cut into 2 equal pieces)
    wood glue or all-purpose white glue
    paint or stain as desired

TOOLS:
    small hack saw or coping saw
    power or hand drill with 3/16" drill bit
    fine grit sandpaper (120 grit or similar)

Cut the dowel rod into two equal pieces for the top and bottom (horizontal) sticks, using the fine toothed coping or hack saw. The 1/4" square pine will have to be cut down from a larger piece, as it is not a standard size. Sometimes scrap pieces are available. The side pieces (1/4" square) are drilled 1/4" from the top and bottom, 1/8" deep using a 3/16" drill bit, on one face only (refer to Diagram 4.5).

Diagram 4.6 shows an exploded view of this type loom, properly laid out and ready to glue.

Place a small drop of glue into each hole, and carefully push the cut dowel rods into place. Make sure the loom opening is even, the same width top and bottom. Wipe off any excess glue, and then set aside to dry (see Diagram 4.7). Construct the loom first and then, after the glue is dry, paint or stain as desired.

4.7 Type 2: Assembled Loom

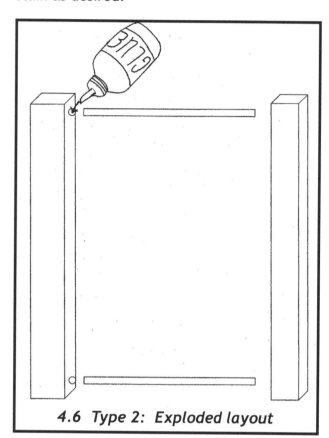

4.6 Type 2: Exploded layout

STAINING OR PAINTING

After the glue has dried, and prior to warping the loom, there is another option to consider. Does the loom have the desired look, or would a little paint or stain add that extra needed touch? The painting can consist of small designs added to the sides (verticals), or painting the entire loom. Keep in mind the colors to be used in the beaded design, and choose a paint color to complement.

The loom can also be stained with any commercial wood stain. A weathered look can be achieved by using a medium stain, allowing it to dry, and then sanding lightly in some areas, and more heavily in others. The 180 grit fine sandpaper works well for this purpose. Any paint and/or stain recommended for wood will work. Whichever is chosen, be sure to follow the directions on the product label, and to clean up everything before starting to bead. Dark stain or paint on white beading thread or beads is a mess best done without.

WARPING THE LOOM

Begin with a thoroughly dry loom! Before warping the loom, the number of "beads per row" must be determined. "Beads per row" refers to the number of beads in a horizontal row, or how many beads wide the pattern will be. The number of warp threads on the loom will equal the number of beads wide <u>plus</u> one more thread (see Diagram 4.8). Each bead is sandwiched between two threads.

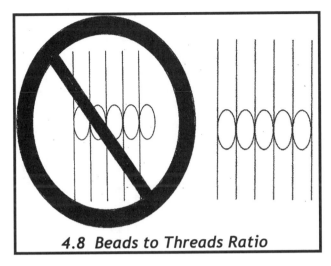

4.8 Beads to Threads Ratio

Tie the "B" Nymo warp thread onto a horizontal stick, using a secure square knot (see Diagram 4.9). For reference purposes, this will become the <u>bottom</u> horizontal stick. There will be a short tail of thread left hanging. Leave it there. Do not glue and trim any knots at this point. Begin warping the loom by going up over the top and down the back of the loom with the warp thread. Go under the bottom horizontal stick, and back over the top again. Keep the warp thread snug, but not stretched tightly. Each row of beads added will tighten the warp slightly, and over-stretching at this point could cause the threads to snap later on. Overstretching could also put too much stress on the glued joints of the loom and could, in time, weaken the entire piece.

Each wrap from bottom to top and back to bottom counts as two (2) threads. Continue warping in this manner, keeping the threads uniformly snug and evenly spaced, until all threads needed for the pattern are on the loom. The amount of space between each warp thread is determined by the size of the beads being used. Be careful not to overlap any threads. The spreader string, discussed below, and the first row of beads will set the correct spacing.

When all warp threads are on the loom, tie off by wrapping the thread around the horizontal stick 3-4 times. Tie a secure square knot. If the desired pattern has an <u>Even</u> number of <u>Beads</u>, there will be an <u>Odd</u> number of <u>Warp</u> threads, and the ending knot will be on the <u>Top</u> horizontal stick (see Diagram 4.10). If there is an <u>Odd</u> number of <u>Beads</u>, there will be an <u>Even</u> number of <u>Warp</u> threads, and the ending knot will be on the <u>Bottom</u> horizontal stick (see Diagram 4.11).

EVEN BEADS = ODD WARP = TOP STICK

ODD BEADS = EVEN WARP = BOTTOM STICK

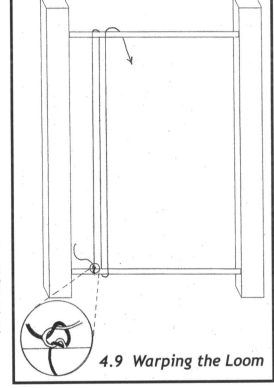

4.9 Warping the Loom

With the loom lying on a flat surface, take note of the location of the warp threads. One-half of the threads will be on the back side (side touching the flat surface) while the other half will be on the front side. In order to bead the pattern using ALL threads, it will be necessary to bring all threads to one working surface. This is done with the spreader string.

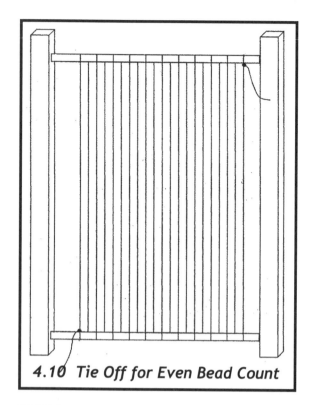

4.10 Tie Off for Even Bead Count

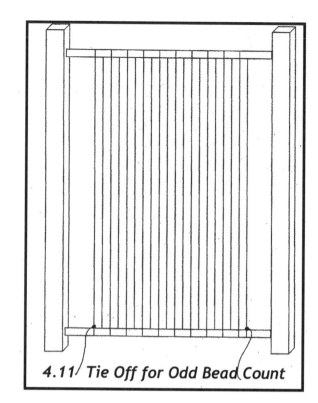

4.11 Tie Off for Odd Bead Count

SPREADER STRING

Cut approximately 12" of "B" Nymo thread. With a secure square knot, tie one end of this thread to a vertical (side) loom stick, 1/2" from the top horizontal stick. This can be worked from right to left, or left to right, depending on personal preference. Thread the free end of the thread onto a #12XL needle, and weave this spreader string Over and Under the warp threads. If the first warp thread is on the "front" side of the loom, the spreader string will go over it. Then bring the spreader string down and under the next thread, which will be on the "back" side of the loom. Continue going over and under, in a weaving fashion, until reaching the other side of the loom. Pull the spreader string taut. Remove the needle, and tie the end of the spreader string onto the side of the loom. (If weaving was started on the left, the string will now be tied off on the right.) Refer to Diagram 4.12 for weaving of the spreader string.

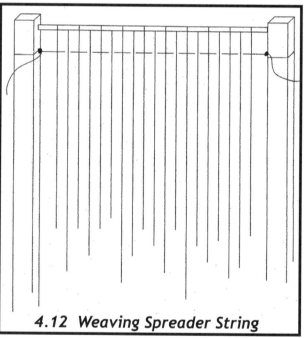

4.12 Weaving Spreader String

All warp threads are now at a single surface. Using a finger, carefully space the warp threads evenly across the top and bottom horizontal sticks, keeping them as straight as possible. The mini-frame loom is now ready for beadweaving. The first row of beads will determine the proper spacing for the warp threads, and further adjustments (if needed) can be made after this first row is on the loom.

5. Beading Technique

CULLING THE BEADS

A look through the beads will show that there are several different sizes and shapes. Even when the hank is marked size 11°, there will still be slight variations. These may not look like much on the hank, but if care isn't taken, the different sizes will give the piece an uneven or lumpy appearance. Compare the beads of all the colors to be used, then determine whether to use the smallest of one color to fit better with the larger of another color. This is called "culling". The finished piece will look better when the beads are carefully culled.

WEFT THREAD

Measure, cut and gently stretch a working length of weft thread. "Working length" refers to the length with which the beader is most comfortable. First-time loom beaders should start with approximately 4-6 feet of thread. Stretching the thread gently will help to remove the "curl" it has acquired from being wrapped around the bobbin, spool or cone. Be careful because the finer threads may snap. Stretch only a small section of thread at a time.

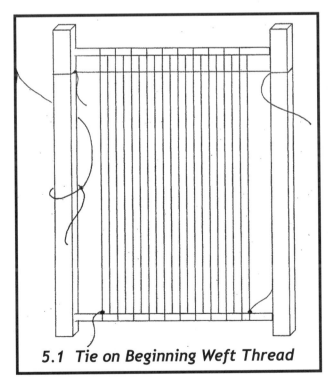

5.1 Tie on Beginning Weft Thread

To help reduce tangling or fraying, apply a thin layer of bee's wax. Lay the thread across the wax. While holding the thread down with the thumb of one hand, gently pull the thread across the wax with the other hand. Pull the thread once or twice through two fingers to remove any excess wax.

Thread the needle. The beading is done with a single strand of thread, which will pass twice through each row of beads. Double the thread, making one end approximately 18 in. longer than the other. Tie the long end loosely onto the side of the loom, leaving a 6" tail (see Diagram 5.1). The thread can be tied onto the left or right side of the loom, depending on personal preference (all diagrams are shown as standard preference for a right-handed person). This knot will be untied later, and the tail of the thread worked back into the loomed piece. The purpose of the knot is to prevent the beads from marching off the end of the thread while the beader is busy aligning the first row of loomwork. More advanced beaders can eliminate this step.

15

CENTERING

To center the picture in the frame, it is best to begin beading in the center. Locate the center horizontal row of the pattern (the patterns in this book have the center row marked). Locate the center of the loom working area by measuring the open space top to bottom, and then dividing by two.

BEGIN BEADWEAVING

Pick up beads in order according to the pattern. When starting from the left side of the mini-frame loom, the pattern will read from left to right. When starting from the right side of the mini-frame loom, the pattern will read from right to left.

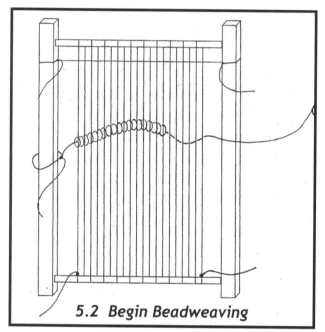

5.2 Begin Beadweaving

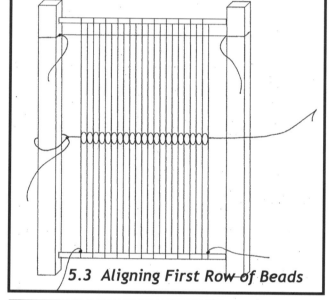

5.3 Aligning First Row of Beads

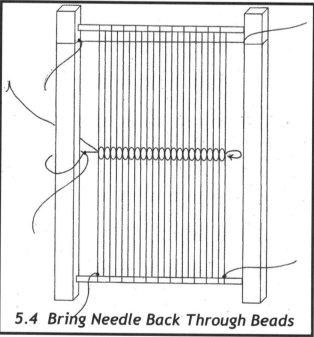

5.4 Bring Needle Back Through Beads

After picking up all the beads for that row, push them all towards the end of the thread. (This is where it comes in handy having the end of the weft thread tied onto the side of the loom.) Pass the needle <u>under</u> all the warp threads, coming up <u>between</u> the <u>last thread</u> and the <u>side of the loom</u> (see Diagram 5.2). Do <u>Not</u> wrap the thread around the outside of the loom.

While holding the weft thread with one hand, use the other hand to lift the beads up between the warp threads (see Diagram 5.3). There will be one bead between each pair of threads, with no beads left over. Hold the beads between the threads with a finger of one hand, and pass the needle and thread back through all the beads with the other hand. Be careful to pass <u>over</u> the warp threads (See Diagrams 5.4 and 5.5).

5.5 Magnified View - Weft Threads Under and Over Warp Threads

After exiting the row of beads, go down between the first warp thread and the side of the loom. The needle and thread are now lined up to pick up the beads for the next row.

It is helpful to mark the pattern as each row is completed, or to use a piece of paper or other straight edge to underline each row as it is being worked. Be careful not to skip or repeat rows. Check the work for errors frequently.

The pattern can be worked from center to top, then center to bottom, or just the reverse. Whichever direction, it should be started in the center, to better place the finished picture in the loom opening.

The beads in each row should be snug, but not so tight that they bunch up. Careful culling and attention to the tension will keep the edges straight.

ADDING NEW WEFT THREAD

As the thread is used up, move the needle up the thread, until it becomes necessary to begin another piece of weft thread. Stop adding rows when approximately 6" of thread remain. Cut, gently stretch and wax another length of weft thread, and thread the needle. Count back three rows of completed beadwork, and enter that row on the side <u>opposite</u> the beginning of each new row. If the pattern is being worked left to right, then enter the row from the right (See Diagram 5.6). Pass through each of the three rows, pulling the tail of the new thread all the way into the beads and out of sight. The needle and thread will end up in position to begin the next new row of beads. The 6" tail remaining from the first thread will be worked in after the beading is complete.

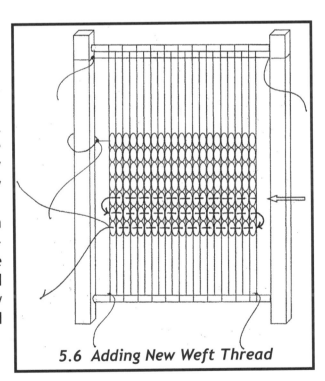

5.6 Adding New Weft Thread

CORRECTING ERRORS

Errors should be corrected when they are found. Check the work frequently. When the last row of loomwork has been completed, double check the entire piece for errors. Now is the time to make any additional corrections, before working in the thread tails. <u>Do</u> <u>not</u> <u>run</u> <u>the</u> <u>needle</u> <u>and</u> <u>thread back</u> <u>through</u> <u>the</u> <u>loomwork</u>. To remove a row of beads, always remove the needle, and carefully pull the thread back through the beads until reaching the error. Return the needle to the thread, and re-weave the rows.

"SHORT NEEDLE SYNDROME"

There are times when it may become necessary to switch to a finer needle. The finer #13 needle is shorter than the #12XL. When working on a wide pattern (size 11° beads, 30 or more beads wide) the needle will not reach all the way across. While holding the beads with one hand, bring the #13 needle back through as many beads as possible. At this point, exit the last bead reached, pull some extra thread out (approximately 2-3"), enter the next bead, and continue across the row to the other side. Pull the thread up snugly, removing the extra loop created by exiting and re-entering in mid row (see Diagram 5.7). Pay extra attention when using this technique to prevent the needle from going under the warp threads instead of over them.

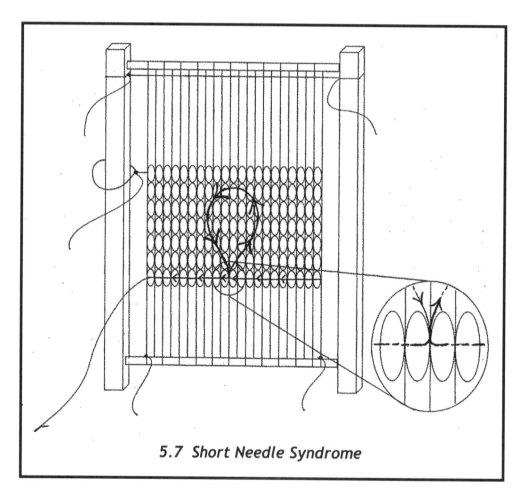

5.7 Short Needle Syndrome

6. FINISHING TOUCHES

When the loomwork is complete, and all errors have been corrected, work the last tail of thread (still on the needle) back into the loomed piece for at least two rows. Exit the row <u>between</u> <u>two</u> <u>beads</u>, not at the edge, and pull the thread up snugly. Carefully trim the thread close to the beads, thus hiding the thread end in the row. Trimming the threads in this manner is safer than taking the thread out to the side of the loomed piece, and trying to trim the weft thread without inadvertently cutting the warp threads (see Diagrams 6.1 and 6.2).

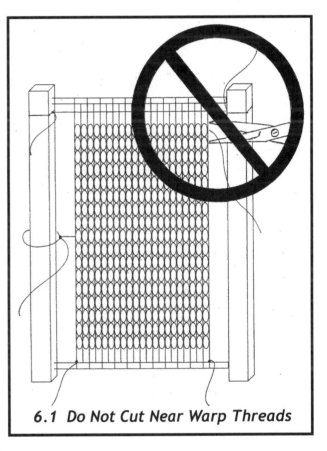

6.1 Do Not Cut Near Warp Threads

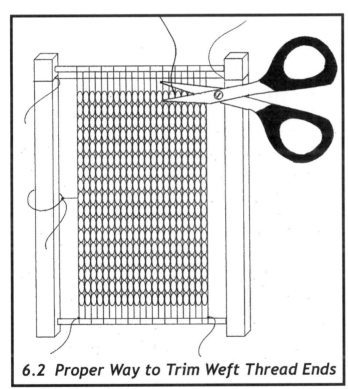

6.2 Proper Way to Trim Weft Thread Ends

All "tail" ends must be worked in and trimmed in the above manner, including the first "tail" that must be untied from the side of the loom.

Carefully cut and remove the spreader string used to hold the warp threads in place. Cut close to the loom, keeping away from the warp threads.

Is the loomwork centered top to bottom <u>and</u> side to side (see Diagram 6.3)? At this point, changing the centering top to bottom is not recommended. Changing the centering side to side can be accomplished to some extent by <u>carefully</u> moving the warp threads across the top and bottom horizontal sticks. If the loomwork appears to be loose in the frame, spread the warp threads apart slightly. This technique will make the loomwork taut.

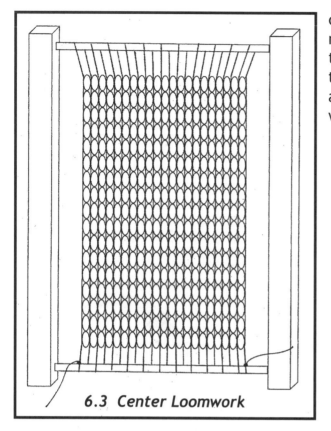
6.3 Center Loomwork

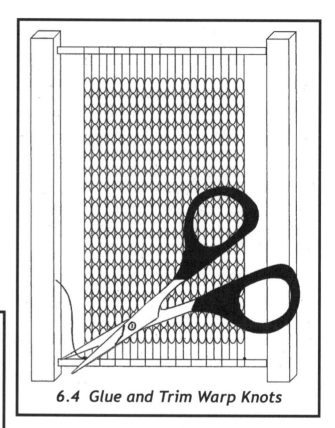
6.4 Glue and Trim Warp Knots

Double check the warp threads to be sure they are evenly spaced. Put a drop of glue on the warp knots, and trim off the excess thread tail (see Diagram 6.4.). The warp threads over the top and bottom horizontal sticks can be left as is, or a <u>very</u> <u>thin</u> layer of glue, e.g., Fray Check™ can be applied to hold them in place (see Diagram 6.5).

6.5 Glue Warp Threads to Horizontal Sticks

7. OTHER IDEAS

The mini-frame loom has been built. The loomwork is complete and all thread tails have been hidden. The warp knots are glued, and the piece is centered. That was a lot of fun. Now what?

What type of picture was done? Is it an ocean theme, a forest theme, a Navajo rug pattern? Any of these, as well as the other patterns in this book, can be just the beginning.

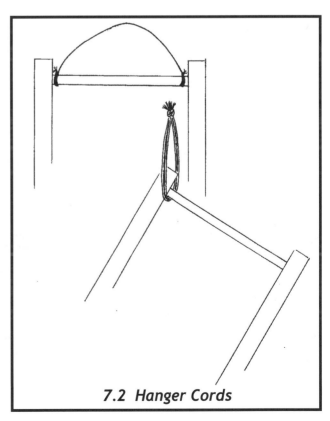

If the "X-lashing" ends were not trimmed during the construction of the mini-frame loom, they can now be used to add finishing touches such as feathers and beads.

Depending on the thickness of the material used for the lashing, use pony or crow beads. Slide the beads up the lashing, out of the way.

Choose a feather and lay the quill over the bottom 1/4" of the lashing (at this point, a small amount of glue can be added). Slide the beads down and cover the area where the feather and the lashing overlap (see Diagram 7.1).

A hanger cord made of ribbon, yarn, leather scrap, etc., can be tied to the top horizontal stick, on either side of the warp threads, turning the framed picture into a suncatcher. It can also be used as an ornament on the holiday tree or as a rear view mirror ornament in a car (see Diagram 7.2).

7.1 Adding Beads and Feathers

7.2 Hanger Cords

A block of aromatic cedar, with holes drilled to accommodate the mini-frame loom "legs" will allow the picture to stand on a dresser or desk, and opens the door to a world of possibilities (see Diagram 7.3).

7.3 Stands: "Orca Joy" Pen Holder

Being in the hospital is never fun, but during the holidays it is especially depressing. Consider the mini-frame loom Christmas Tree, Snowman, Santa or Candle patterns. One or more of these, mounted on a block of wood, with miniature wrapped packages and a little glitter snow would go a long way to cheer up a sick child of any age.

Modify the "Old Fashioned Sampler" pattern to spell out a personal message. All the letters are there. Transfer them to the beading grid paper or add them to a pattern from this book. Because the space is limited, a little ingenuity is required.

Don't forget the birth announcements. Many people have the embroidered or printed ones framed and hanging in the baby's room. How unique to have one of beadwork, mounted on a base or hanging on the wall. Refer to the lettering and numbers shown in the "Old Fashioned Sampler". Add the baby's name and birthday to the "Cradleboard" or the "Bear Paw" pattern.

Sculpture doesn't necessarily require a large chunk of marble. Sculpture is also building. Sculpture is the art of creating three-dimensional figures. As an example, refer to the "Orca

7.4 "Orca Joy" Sculpture

Joy" in Diagram 7.4. This sculpture was constructed of driftwood, purchased and gathered seashells, coral, urchins and sea stars. In addition to the fun of constructing this work, it also took two blue ribbons at the local county fair.

Create smaller sculptures using one or two mini-frame loom pictures, driftwood, special stones, beads, feathers and whatever else strikes the fancy. Examples of other sculptures can be seen in Diagrams 7.5, 7.6 and 7.7.

In addition to adding the mini-frame loomed picture to a sculpture, try adding things to the mini-frame loomed picture. Small crystal beads can be added to "Crystal Angel" by actually sewing a small crystal over the top of the existing bead. Hide all thread ends in the loomed work, and carefully trim.

7.5 "1-800-2 HELP ME" Sculpture

7.6 "Jammin" Sculpture

7.7 "Just For Fun" Sculpture

23

Fringe can also be added to pieces left on the loom, such as has been done with the "Knife Sheath". Add the fringe <u>after</u> all loom beading has been completed, and the thread ends are hidden and trimmed. Add the fringe by running a threaded needle through an entire row of loomed work. Pick up the required number of beads. Use a turnaround bead to go back up the fringe (just go back through all but the last bead) and back through the same loomed row. Pass the needle and thread through the <u>next</u> row of loomed work and add the next fringe in the same manner.

Consider constructing a mini-frame loom to accommodate a slightly different project, one that can be removed from the loom. Two suggestions are loomed strips for hair barrettes and loomed "patches" to be stitched onto clothing or accessories. In the pattern section are pattern ideas for barrettes, including a special pattern for the author's favorite "Firebird" using Japanese 15° hex beads.

To construct the mini-frame loom for a barrette (or any project that will be removed from the loom), determine the finished length of the piece. Allow enough center area for that measurement, plus 1-1/2" on either end. For a loomed piece 5 inches long, the opening would be a <u>minimum</u> of 8 inches. This added space allows for end weaving, cutting and tying off. The width of the loom center opening should be sufficient to clear the side pieces when passing the needle through the beads. While the measurements may be different, the construction technique will be the same.

These same barrette patterns can be the starting point for a longer loomed strip that can be worked on a full-size beading loom. The finished strip can be attached to belts, leggings, shirts or moccasins. These patterns can also be used for hatbands, whether attached to a leather backing or not.

There are as many pattern ideas as there are people to design them. Let this little book be a jumping off point, and...

LET   THE   IMAGINATION   TAKE   FLIGHT! ! !

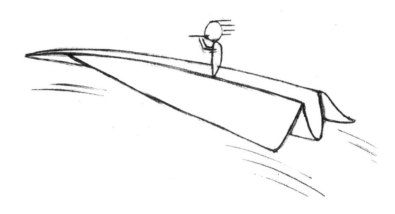

A. PATTERNS

The following patterns have been designed using numbers to represent bead colors. Each pattern has a table indicating the CODE (pattern reference), COLOR (bead color and type) and COUNT. The COUNT refers to the actual number of beads used in the pattern, but does not allow for culling. Depending upon the quality of the beads, increase the COUNT by 25-50%.

For example, the "Bird" pattern calls for 554 crystal/white lined 11^0 seed beads. To allow for culling, multiply 554 by 25% (554 x .25 = 138.5) Add these 138 beads to the 554 actual count (554 + 138 = 692). The minimum number of crystal/white lined 11^0 seed beads recommended for the "Bird" pattern is 692. Yes, there will be beads left-over. Save them for another project. It is always better to have too many beads than too few.

The colors shown in these patterns are suggestions, not demands. Experiment with different colors. Whichever color combination is chosen, it is best to use felt pens or colored pencils to color the pattern before beading. The colorized pattern is easier to follow.

The patterns are also marked with the recommended mini-loom size. This loom size is based upon the size of beads used, as well as the finished length and width of the loomed piece. Remember: When the piece is to be removed from the loom, as for a barrette, the loom length must be increased accordingly. Add at least 1-1/2" top and bottom to allow for end-weaving and tying off.

1. Barn Owl

```
11111011111110011111111101110011111
10011111111663663636363631110111011
11011101136366636663663636333111011001
11111113336363666336363633363333101111
01111133333363336366366633333111001
11103334334444343663434444334333311111
00113334545554555333544555455553331011
11133354666666666653566666666654333011
10133546666666666656666666666663533101
01133546666666666664666666666663533111
11133456666666666664666666666664533100
11025466677766666646666667776666542111
11024526667776666664666667776662452111
11125522333366666646666663333322542111
11124522222236666646666663222222542101
00125442222223666646666632222222452111
11124522222222366646663222222222452111
11122522222222366646663222222225524001   —CENTER
01122542222222366646663222222224523111
10122544222222266545662222222245222311
11122255422222225444522222222445222331
01122225442222224434422222224552226333
11322222255422222443442222244522623322
13222222225544222243422224545226336222
13222222225454442224222444552623626222
32622222225544322223343552263326222
23232222222222254444343452222322322222
23332622222222222222222222263363222222
22633632222222222222222222623323222222
22222333232222222222226222232622222222
22222236326262222262262223222222226222
22222222623622262262226622262222222222
22222222622332322326223332222222222222
22222222222223323262232322226222222222
22622222222262232332332222222222222222
22222222222222222222222222222222222222
```

MINI-LOOM SIZE:

3" wide x 4" long (center opening)

BEADS
size 11° seed beads

CODE	COLOR	COUNT
0	peridot trans luster	39
1	kelly green trans luster	169
2	crystal/white lined	526
3	light topaz trans	177
4	topaz trans	93
5	dark topaz trans	72
6	grey trans luster	244
7	black opaque	12

THREAD

SIZE	COLOR	LENGTH
O	white	5 yards
B	white	6 yards

NEEDLES

#12 extra long
#13

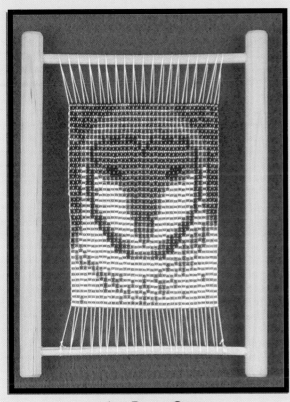

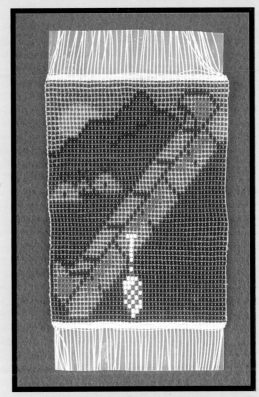

1. Barn Owl

3. Birchbark Canoe

2. BearPaw

4. Bird

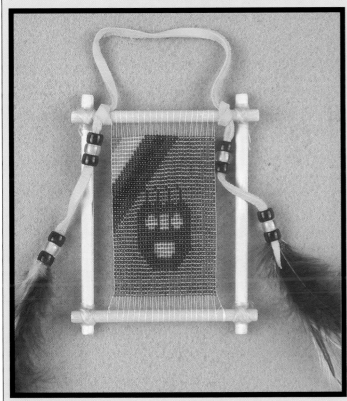

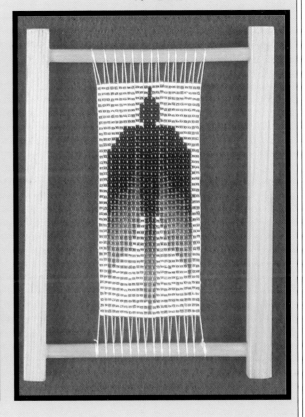

5. CINNAMON BUN

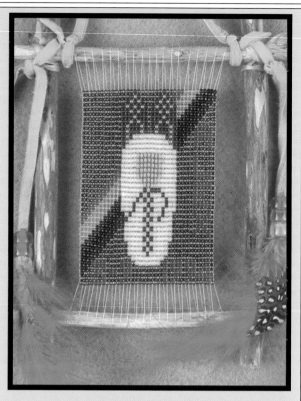

6. CRADLEBOARD

7. DOUBLE RAINBOW

9. END OF TRAIL

8. EARTHTONE GEOMETRIC

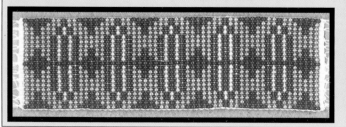

2. BEARPAW

```
1111222233334444555566667777777777777
1112222333344445555666677777777777777
1122223333444455556666777777777777777
1222233334444555566667777777777777777
2222333344445555666677777777777777777
2223333444455556666777777777777777777
2233334444555566667777777777777777777
2333344445555666677777777777777777777
3333444455556666777777777777777777777
3334444555566667777777777777777777777
3344445555666677777777777777777777777
3444455556666777777777777777777777777
4444555566667777777777777777777777777
4445555666687778777877787777777777777
4455556666778777877787778777777777777
4555566667778777877787778777777777777
5555666677787778777877787777777777777
5556666777788878887888788877777777777
5566667777888888888888888887777777777
5666677778888888888888888888877777777
6666777788889988999889988887777777777
6667777788899998999899998887777777777
6677777788899998999899998887777777777
6777777788889988999889988887777777777
7777777788888888888888888887777777777
7777777788888888888888888887777777777
7777777788888888888888888887777777777
7777777788888899999998888887777777777
7777777788888899999998888887777777777
7777777788888899999998888877777777777
7777777777888889999988887777777777777
7777777777788888888888887777777777777
7777777777778888888888877777777777777
7777777777778888888887777777777777777
7777777777777777777777777777777777777
7777777777777777777777777777777777777
7777777777777777777777777777777777777
7777777777777777777777777777777777777
7777777777777777777777777777777777777
7777777777777777777777777777777777777
7777777777777777777777777777777777777
```

CENTER —

BEADS
size 11° seed beads

CODE	COLOR	COUNT
1	garnet trans	10
2	orange trans	26
3	yellow trans	42
4	emerald trans	58
5	cobalt blue trans	74
6	amethyst trans	90
7	light sapphire trans	923
8	dark smoke topaz trans	232
9	light topaz	62

THREAD

SIZE	COLOR	LENGTH
O	white	5 yards
B	white	6 yards

NEEDLES

#12 extra long
#13

MINI-LOOM SIZE

3" wide x 4" long (center opening)

```
1111111111111111111111111111111111111111111111111
1111111111111111111111111111111111111111111111111
111111111111111111111111122211111111111333333111111
11111111111111111111111112444211111111113555555531111
111111111111111111111111124444421111111135555666653111
111111177777111111111122444444421111113335566665531111
1111177777777771111124444444442222111133566665535511
111177777777777771112444444444424444221135366663535555
11177777777222222244444444442444444421355355355555
1117777777244444444444442224444444443555353555555
111777777724444444444444244444444444435333335355555
111177772444444444444222244444444443555555355535555
11111224444444444424444444444443555553566653554
1111244444444444442244444444444435555535565555344
111244444444444444444444444444435555535666555444
2224444444444444444444444444435555535365555544444
44444444444444444444444443555553566655554444444
44444444444444444444444443533333556655355444444
4444444444443434444444444435555535666555554444444
444444443434444434444444443555553555555554444444
4443434444344445554444444435555535555555554444444
4444344435344555554444443555555353355555554444444
4445554355535555355544435555535555355554444444444
4455555535355555555443555553565553554444444444
45555355533333444444435333335565553444444444444
5555555555444444444435555535666555544444444444444  ── CENTER
44444444444444444443555553555655555444444444444444
888888888444444443555553566655554444444444444444
4444444888444488835555353565555884444444444444444
444444448888888355555356665555588888884444444444
44444444444444435555535566535554448888888888888
444444444444443535333355666555344444488888888888
444444444444443555535555555554444444488888888888
444444444443555553559995554444444444444888888888
44444444443555553555595554444444444444448888888888
444444444435555535355595544444444444444488888888
888888888355555355535595888888888888888888888888
8888888835555353655535598888888888888888888888888
83338888353333355655553988888888888888888888888
35533335555535666555586888888888888844444444444
35553555555535565555588898888888884444444444444
3555553333335666555544464444444444444444444444
356666555353655555449994444444444444444444444
35666655356665555449996944444444444444444444
35666653556553554449969644444444444444444444444
35666635556555344449696944444444444444444444
43555353555555544444696964444444444444444444
443535555555554444449696944444444444444444444
44435555555554444444696994444444444444444444
444435555555444444446994444444444444444444444
4444455555444444444494444444444444444444444
444444444444444444444444444444444444444444444
```

MINI-LOOM SIZE

3-1/2" wide x 4-1/2" long (center opening)
3-1/2" wide x 7-1/2" long if removing piece from loom

BEADS
size 12° seed beads

CODE	COLOR	COUNT
1	light blue trans	272
2	dark green trans	50
3	dark topaz trans	181
4	light green trans	1142
5	topaz trans	503
6	garnet trans	94
7	citrine (yellow) trans	53
8	medium blue trans	220
9	Navajo white pearl	33

THREAD

SIZE	COLOR	LENGTH
O	white	8 yards
B	white	8 yards

NEEDLES

#12 extra long
#13

4. BIRD

```
11111111111111111111111111
11111111111121111111111111
11111111111121111111111111
11111111111221111111111111
11111111111222221111111111
11111111111222221111111111
11111111111222221111111111
11111111111221111111111111
11111222222222222111111111
11111222322222322221111111
11112222232222232222211111
11122222232222232222221111
11222222232222232222222211
11222222232222232222222211
11222222232222232222222211
11222222232222232222222211
11222222342222243222222211
11222223342222243322222211
11222223452222254322222211
11222333452222254333222211
```
CENTER ─
```
11223344563222365443322211
11233444563222365444332211
11234455673222376554432211
11344555671323176555443311
11345566771333177665543311
11455666711333117766655411
11456677711434117776655411
11566777111444111777665511
11566777111444111777765511
11677711111545111177776611
11677111111555111117761611
11771111111555111111771111
11711111111656111111111711
11711111111666111111111711
11111111111666111111111111
11111111111767111111111111
11111111111777111111111111
11111111111777111111111111
11111111111171111111111111
11111111111171111111111111
11111111111111111111111111
```

MINI-LOOM SIZE

3" wide by 4" long (center opening)

BEADS
size 11° seed beads

CODE	COLOR	COUNT
1	crystal/white lined	554
2	cobalt blue transparent	233
3	light sapphire transparent luster	57
4	garnet transparent	41
5	dark hyacinth (orange) transparent	41
6	hyacinth (orange) transparent	41
7	citrine (yellow) transparent	58

THREAD

SIZE	COLOR	LENGTH
O	white	4 yards
B	white	5 yards

NEEDLES

#12 extra long
#13

```
11111111111111111111111111111111111111
11111111113111111111111111111111111111
11111111133331111111111111111111111111
11111111333331111111111111111111111111
11111111333331111111111111111111111111
11111111333331511111111111111111111111
11111115533355111111111111111111111111
11111151155551111111111111199111111111
11111111515111151111118881199911111111
11111111111511555511118998199911111111
11111111111515555111118998199911111111
11111111111515555111118998199911111111
11111111111515555111118998199911111111
11111111111515551111118987777911111111
11111111111155111111111889999999111111
11111111111151111111111198998899911111
11111111111151111111111199986689991111
11111155515111111111111199998889999111
11111555515111111111111199999997997111
11115111551111111111199999979999771111
1111111111151155511119999999788991111111  ← CENTER
11111111111515555599999999999981111111
11111111111551199999999799999988111111
11111111111519999999999997999999811111111
11111111111599999999999997999999811111
11111111111999999999999997999998111111
11111111199999999999999997999991111111
22222229999999999999999997999111111111
22222222999999999999999999799222111111
22222229999999999999999999972222222211
22222222999999999777779998772242222222
22222229999999999999997887722444222222
22222229999999999999998222224442222222
22222222999999999999992222222522242222
22222222799999999999992222552525244422
22222227799999999999922222225552442222
22222227779999999979999222225222522522
222220000007777997799999222225252522
22222222222222222222222222222222225255522
22222222222222222222222222222222225222
```

MINI-LOOM SIZE

3" wide by 4" long (center opening)

5. CINNAMON BUN

BEADS
size 11° seed beads

CODE	COLOR	COUNT
1	light sapphire trans luster	675
2	peridot trans	235
3	garnet trans	22
4	deep amethyst trans	14
5	dark kelly green trans	79
6	black opaque	2
7	dark smoke topaz trans	43
8	light topaz trans	33
9	dark topaz trans	334
0	white opal	6

THREAD

SIZE	COLOR	LENGTH
O	white	5 yards
B	white	6 yards

NEEDLES

#12 extra long

32

6. CRADLEBOARD

```
1111111111111121111111211144556677889
1111111111111232111112321445566778899
1111111111112323211123232455667788991
1111111111123232321232323256677889911
1111111111122323221223232266778899111
1111111111122232221222322267788991111
1111111111122323221223232277889911111
1111111111123222321232223278899111111
1111111111123222324232223288991111111
1111111111123200000000023289911111111
1111111111123000000000003299111111111
1111111111120000000000000291111111111
1111111111100000000000000011111111111
1111111111100000000000000011111111111
1111111111100000θθ00000000011111111111
1111111111100000θθ00000000011111111111
1111111111100000θθ00000000011111111111
1111111111400000θθ00000000011111111111
1111111114400000θθ00000000011111111111
111111114450000000θθ0000000011111111111
1111111445500000000θθ000000011111111111
111111445560000000202220000111111111111
11111445566000000202000200011111111111
1111445566700002020θ20002001111111111111
111445566770002000200020011111111111
11445566778000200202002000111111111111
144556677890200002000200011111111111
445566778899200002θ2020001111111111111
455667788992000000200000011111111111
556677889911000002θ2000001111111111111
566778899111000000200000011111111111
667788991111000002θ2000001111111111111
677889911111000002000001111111111111
778899111111100002θ20001111111111111
788991111111100000200001111111111111
889911111111100000000011111111111111
899111111111110000000111111111111111
991111111111111111111111111111111111
911111111111111111111111111111111111
111111111111111111111111111111111111
111111111111111111111111111111111111
```

CENTER

MINI-LOOM SIZE
3" wide by 4" long (center opening)

BEADS
size 11⁰ seed beads

CODE	COLOR	COUNT
1	light sapphire trans luster	777
2	dark brown matte	116
3	copper supra (metallic)	34
4	garnet trans	32
5	hyacinth (orange) trans	33
6	citrine (yellow) trans	37
7	emerald trans	41
8	cobalt (blue) trans	44
9	deep amethyst trans	46
0	white opal	270
θ	Cheyenne pink	50
	OR blue pearl matte	

THREAD

SIZE	COLOR	LENGTH
O	white	5 yards
B	white	6 yards

NEEDLES
#12 extra long

33

7. DOUBLE RAINBOW

```
7888881888881 8888188
7781888881 8888188888
6778188188888888 81888
6677888881 81818888818
5667781888888888 81 8888
5566778818181 88888888
4556677888888888 188188
4455667781 8881 8888888
3445566778818888 81818
3344556677 8818888 8888
2334455667 78888881 8888
2233445566778888 88188
82233445566778 8188818
88223344556677 8888888
888223344556677 881888
1888223344556677 88888
8888822334455667 78188
8818882233445566 77888
888888223344556677 88
8188181822334455 66778
8888888822334455 6677
1818818822334455 5667
8888888888223344 5566
8188188881882233 44556
8888881 8888182233 4455
7881888888888822 33445
7788888188188882 23344
6778188888888818 22334
6677888881888888 82233 ━ CENTER
5667788888881 881 8818223
5566778188818 88888822
4556677888888 88188882
4455667788188 88888888
3445566778888 81888888
3344556677888 8888 1818
2334455667788 18888888
2233445566778 8881 8188
8223344556677 88888888
8822334455667 78188888
888223344556677 881818
8888223344556677 88888
8188822334455667 78188
88888822334455667 888
188888223344556677 88
888881882233445566778
8818888822334455 6677
88888888 8822334455667
88888818888223344 5566
8188888888 8822334455 6
88818888888882233 4455
8888888818888 2233445
18888188888888 8223344
8818888888818 81882 2334
88888188888888 8882233
88818888888881 88818223
88888888818 8888888822
81888888888888 81881882
```

<table>
<tr><td colspan="3" align="center">BEADS
size 11° seed beads</td></tr>
<tr><td><u>CODE</u></td><td><u>COLOR</u></td><td><u>COUNT</u></td></tr>
<tr><td>1</td><td>crystal rainbow</td><td>89</td></tr>
<tr><td>2</td><td>garnet trans</td><td>84</td></tr>
<tr><td>3</td><td>hyacinth (orange) trans luster</td><td>84</td></tr>
<tr><td>4</td><td>citrine (yellow) trans</td><td>84</td></tr>
<tr><td>5</td><td>emerald trans</td><td>84</td></tr>
<tr><td>6</td><td>cobalt (blue) trans</td><td>84</td></tr>
<tr><td>7</td><td>amethyst trans</td><td>84</td></tr>
<tr><td>8</td><td>medium sapphire trans</td><td>604</td></tr>
</table>

THREAD

SIZE	COLOR	LENGTH
O	white	4 yards
B	white	4 yards

NEEDLES

#12 extra long

MINI-LOOM SIZE
3" wide by 8" long (center opening)

8. EARTHTONE GEOMETRIC

```
233333333323333333332
223333333222333333322
222233322222223332222
223333333222333333322
233333333323333333332
333344444444444443333
334411111121111114433
441122222222222221144
334411111121111114433
333344444444444443333
233333333323333333332
223333333222333333322
222233322222223332222
223333333222333333322
233333333323333333332
333344444444444443333
334411111121111114433
441122222222222221144
334411111121111114433
333344444444444443333
233333333323333333332
223333333222333333322
222233322222223332222
223333333222333333322
233333333323333333332
333344444444444443333
334411111121111114433
```
CENTER → `441122222222222221144`
```
334411111121111114433
333344444444444443333
233333333323333333332
223333333222333333322
222233322222223332222
223333333222333333322
233333333323333333332
333344444444444443333
334411111121111114433
441122222222222221144
334411111121111114433
333344444444444443333
233333333323333333332
223333333222333333322
222233322222223332222
223333333222333333322
233333333323333333332
333344444444444443333
334411111121111114433
441122222222222221144
334411111121111114433
333344444444444443333
233333333323333333332
223333333222333333322
222233322222223332222
223333333222333333322
233333333323333333332
```

MINI-LOOM SIZE
3" wide by 7-1/2" long (center opening)

BEADS
size 11º seed beads

CODE	COLOR	COUNT
1	light topaz trans	140
2	dark smoke topaz trans	285
3	peridot trans luster	540
4	kelly green trans	190

THREAD

SIZE	COLOR	LENGTH
O	white	4 yards
B	white	4 yards

NEEDLES

#12 extra long

9. END OF TRAIL

```
1111111111111111111111111111111111111111111111
1222222222222222222222222222222222222222222221
1222222222222222222222222222222222222232222221
1222222222222222222222222222222222222342222221
1222222222222222222222222222222222223252222221
1222222222222222222233333222222222223226222221
1222222222222222223333333333322222234223222221
1222222222222222232233333333332222232522222221
1222222222222222223233333333332223226222222221
1222222222222222232223332233333234223222222221
1222222222222222222222222333333325222222222221
1222222222222222222222233333333326222222222221
1222222222222222222222233333333323222222222221
1222222222222222222222333333333322222222222221
1222222222222222222223333333333322222222222221
1222222222222222222333333333333322222222222221
1222222222222222233333333333333333333322221
1222222222222223333333333333333333333333221
1222222222222233333333333333333333333333321
1222222222223333333333333333333333333333321
1222222222233333333333333333333333333333321
1222222223333333333333333333333333333333321
1222222233333333333333333333333333333333321
1222333333333333333333333333333322333333333221    ┤CENTER
1223333333333333333333333333222233333333321
1333333333333333333333333333222222333333322221
1223333333333222323333333333222222223333333322221
1223333333332223422223333333222222223333333322221
1223333333322232522222333332222222233333333322221
1223333333223226222222333332222332233333332222221
1223333333234223222233333333222233223333332222221
1223333332325222222222333323322222233333222222221
1223333323226222222222233323322223333222222222221
1222233334223222222222233323322233332222222222221
1222222325222222222222233323322233322222222222221
1222223226222222222222233333333333333332222222221
1222224223222222222233333333333333333322222221
1222225222222222222333333333333333333333332221
1222226222222222233333333333333333333333333221
1222223222222233333333333333333333333333333321
1222222222223333333333333333333333333333333331
1222222222233333333333333333333333333333333331
1222222223333333333333333333333333333333333331
1222223333333333333333333333333333333333333331
1233333333333333333333333333333333333333333331
1111111111111111111111111111111111111111111111
```

MINI-LOOM SIZE
3" wide by 4" long (center opening)

BEADS
size 13° seed beads

CODE	COLOR	COUNT
1	aqua trans	182
2	grey trans	1047
3	black opaque	912
4	garnet trans	7
5	orange trans	7
6	yellow trans	7

THREAD

SIZE	COLOR	LENGTH
O	white	6 yards
B	white	7 yards

NEEDLES

#13

36

11. Fire Colors

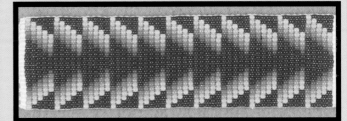

12. Firebird

14. Geometric

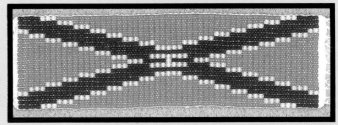

15. Gone Fishin'

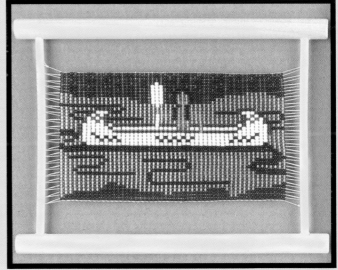

10. Fancy Dancer

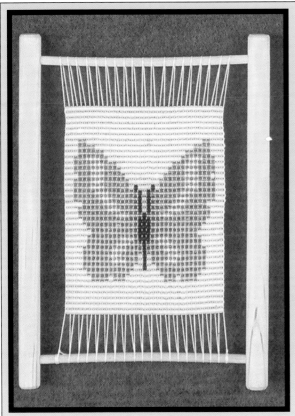

13. Fringed Knife Sheath

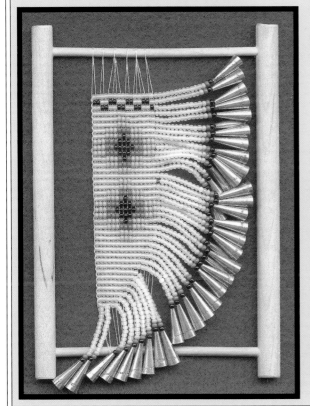

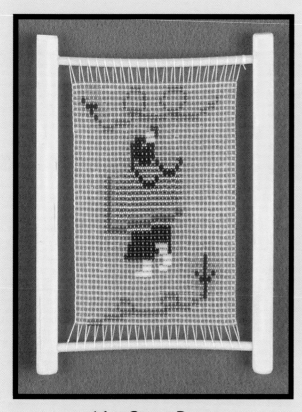

16. GOTTA DANCE

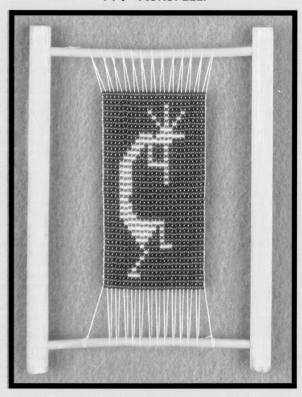

17. HEARTBEAT OF THE PEOPLE

18. JAMMIN'

19. KOKOPELLI

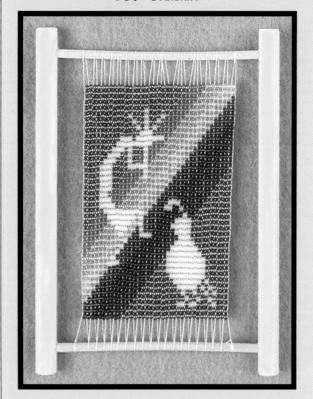

10. FANCY DANCER

```
1111111111111111111111111111111111111111111
1111111111111111111111111111111111111111111
1111111111111111111111111111111111111111111
1111111111111111111111111111111111111111111
1111111111111111111111111111111111111111111
1111111111111111111111111111111111111111111
1112211111111111111111111111111122111
1112222111111111111111111111112222111
1112222221111111111111111111222222111
1122244221111111111111111122244222 11
1122224442211111111111112224442222 11
112222444222211111111112222444222211
1112224442222211111111222224442 22111
112222444422222211111122222244422 2211
112222444422222215111512222244422 2211
112222224442222222515222222244422 2211
112222224442222222515222222444222 2211
111122222444222222515222224442 2222111
1112222222244422225152222444222 2222111
1112222222224442225222444222 2222222111
1111222222222222225555222222222222221111
1111122233333333355533333333322211111
1111112333333333335553333333332111111
1111133333334443555344433333333311111
1111133333334443335333444333333 311111
1111133333334443333353333444 333333331111
111133333344433315133334 4433333331111
1111333333344433315133 33444333333331111
111133333333333331151 13333333333331111
1111133333333333311111113333 3333311111
111113333133311111111113331 3333111111
1111111111111111111111111111111111111111111
1111111111111111111111111111111111111111111
1111111111111111111111111111111111111111111
1111111111111111111111111111111111111111111
1111111111111111111111111111111111111111111
1111111111111111111111111111111111111111111
```

CENTER (marker at left of chart)

MINI-LOOM SIZE
3" wide by 4" long (center opening)

BEADS
size 11° seed beads

CODE	COLOR	COUNT
1	white opal	781
2	hyacinth (orange) trans	268
3	citrine (yellow) trans	196
4	crystal aurora borealis (AB)	96
5	black matte	28

THREAD

SIZE	COLOR	LENGTH
O	white	5 yards
B	white	6 yards

NEEDLES

#12 extra long

39

11. FIRE COLORS

```
123456666666666654321
612345666666666543216
661234566666665432166
666123456666654321666
666612345666543216666
123456666666666654321
612345666666666543216
661234566666665432166
666123456666654321666
666612345666543216666
123456666666666654321
612345666666666543216
661234566666665432166
666123456666654321666
666612345666543216666
123456666666666654321
612345666666666543216
661234566666665432166
666123456666654321666
666612345666543216666
123456666666666654321
612345666666666543216
661234566666665432166 ──CENTER
666123456666654321666
666612345666543216666
123456666666666654321
612345666666666543216
661234566666665432166
666123456666654321666
666612345666543216666
123456666666666654321
612345666666666543216
661234566666665432166
666123456666654321666
666612345666543216666
123456666666666654321
612345666666666543216
661234566666665432166
666123456666654321666
666612345666543216666
123456666666666654321
612345666666666543216
661234566666665432166
666123456666654321666
666612345666543216666
```

MINI-LOOM SIZE
3" wide by 8" long (center opening)

BEADS
size 11° seed beads

CODE	COLOR	COUNT
1	yellow opaque	110
2	pumpkin opaque	110
3	orange opaque	110
4	red opaque	110
5	brick opaque	110
6	cobalt blue opaque	605

THREAD

SIZE	COLOR	LENGTH
O	white	4 yards
B	white	4 yards

NEEDLES

#12 extra long

12. FIREBIRD

BEADS
size 15° Japanese hex beads

CODE	COLOR	COUNT
1	turquoise opaque	794
2	yellow opaque	148
3	orange opaque	123
4	red opaque	113
5	cobalt (blue) opaque	354
6	brick opaque	22

THREAD

SIZE	COLOR	LENGTH
O	white	4 yards
B	white	4 yards

NEEDLES

#12 extra long
#13

MINI-LOOM SIZE

3" wide by 7-1/2" long (center opening)

```
11121111112111111112111
11232111123211111123211
12343211234321112343221
23454322345432223454332
34525433452543345254333
45232544523254452323254
52343255234325552343325
45232544523254452323254
34525433452543345254333
23454322345432223454332
12343211234321112343221
11232111123211111123211
11121111112111111112111
11111111111111111111111
11111111111111111111111
11111111111111111111111
11111111111111111111111
11111111151111111111111
11111111151111111111111
11111111151111111111111
11111111555111111111111
11111111555111111111111
11111111555111111111111
11155555155515555511111
11555555155515555555511
15555555155515555555551
55555555555555555555555
55555555555555555555555
55555555555555555555555
55555555555555555555555
55234655555555643255
52346551555555515564325
23465511555555511556432
34655111255521115564433
46551111355531111555644
65551111422241111555556
55551111633361111115555
55551111544451111115555
55111111566651111111555
55111111555551111111155
51111111555551111111115
51111111555551111111115
11111111555551111111111
11111111255521111111111
11111111355531111111111
11111111422241111111111
11111111633361111111111
11111111544451111111111
11111111566651111111111
11111111555551111111111
11111111555551111111111
11111111555551111111111
11111111555551111111111
11111111555111111111111
11111111555111111111111
11111111555111111111111
11111111151111111111111
Continued on Left
```

CENTER →

Firebird Continued

```
11111111111111111111111
11111111111111111111111
11111111111111111111111
11111111111111111111111
11121111112111111112111
11232111123211111123211
12343211234321112343221
23454322345432223454332
34525433452543345254333
45232544523254452323254
52343255234325552343325
45232544523254452323254
34525433452543345254333
23454322345432223454332
12343211234321112343221
11232111123211111123211
11121111112111111112111
```

13. FRINGED KNIFE SHEATH

```
11111111111111
22112211221221
11221122112112
11111111111111
11111333111111
11111333111111
11133344333111
11133342433331111
333444222444333
333442222244333
333444222444333
11133342433331111
11133344333111
11111333111111
11111333111111
11111111111111
11111333111111
11111333111111
11133344333111
11133342433331111 ———— CENTER
333444222444333
333442222244333
333444222444333
11133342433331111
11133344433311
11111133311111
11111113331111
11111111111111
111111111111
111111111111
11111111111
1111111111
1111111111
111111111
11111111
1111111
11111
1111
111
```

MINI-LOOM SIZE
3" wide by 4" long
(center opening)

BEADS
size 11° seed beads

CODE	COLOR	COUNT
1	white opal	304
2	black opaque	41
3	turquoise opaque	108
4	red opaque	52

FRINGE *

1	white opal	492
2	black opaque	82
3	turquoise opaque	41
4	red opaque	41

THREAD

SIZE	COLOR	LENGTH
O	white	4 yards
B	white	5-7** yards

NEEDLES

#12 extra long
#13

* Fringe is 12 white, 1 turquoise, 1 red, 1 black and one 1/2" silver cone, using another black as a turn around bead. Fringe each of the 39 rows and then add two more at the bottom of the loomed piece.

** If fringe is added

14. GEOMETRIC

```
11123333333333333332111
11123333333333333332111
11112333333333333321111
11112333333333333321111
21112333333333333321112
21111233333333333211112
21111233333333333211112
32111233333333333211123
32111123333333332111123
32111123333333332111123
33211123333333332111233
33211112333333321111233
33211112333333321111233
33321112333333321112333
33321111233321111123333
33321111233321111123333
33332111233321111233333
33332111123211111233333
33332111123211111233333
33333211123211112333333
33333211112111112333333
33333211112111112333333
33333321112111123333333
33333321111111123333333
33333321121211123333333
33333332121212123333333
33333332121212123333333
33333332122212123333333
33333332121212123333333
33333332121212123333333
33333321121211123333333
33333321111111123333333
33333321112111123333333
33333211112111112333333
33333211112111112333333
33333211123211112333333
33332111123211111233333
33332111123211111233333
33332111233321111233333
33321111233321111123333
33321111233321111123333
33321112333332111112333
33211112333332111111233
33211112333333321111233
33211112333333321111233
32111112333333332111123
32111112333333332111123
32111123333333332111123
21111233333333332111112
21111233333333332111112
21112333333333333321112
11112333333333333321111
11112333333333333321111
11123333333333333332111
11123333333333333332111
```

CENTER

BEADS
size 11° seed beads

CODE	COLOR	COUNT
1	black opaque	370
2	white opal	195
3	red opaque	590

THREAD

SIZE	COLOR	LENGTH
O	white	4 yards
B	white	4 yards

NEEDLES
#12 extra long

MINI-LOOM SIZE
3" wide by 7-1/2" long (center opening)

15. GONE FISHIN'

```
11111111222223322322222222232223322444444
54444444422223232323222222233322332244444
54454444222223232323222222233333233222244444
45444442222232231111222332233233222224444
11111122222232116666663332232332222224444
11111122222223166666666633222332332222224444
5444442222221676668666332232332222224444
4544442222216767666686633222333222222222224444
11111122222166766666686332222232222222224444
11111112222216111166686633222222222222222244
4454444222211122161666863322222222222222244
11111112222223222161686633222222222222222224
5444444222223222161668663222222222222222224
11111112222223222161666633222222222222322444
4445444422222322216166663322222222222324444
5444544422222322216166663322222222222324444
4544454442222222216166663322222222222324444
11111111122222221616666332222222222324444
11111111122222221616666332222222222322444
54444544444222999999966663322222222222322444
45445444442299921616666332222222222322444
11111188882999221616866332222222222322444
44445889998888899916686332223322222322444
4544489999999999991686633222322322222322444
1111188999899999991686633223223222322444
54444588882888821616866332232232222322444 ◄CENTER
4544444544229922161668663322232232222322244
5444454444229992161668663322322232222322444
111166666229922161668663322322322222322444
445666666669966666168663322322322222322444
1111666666222221616666332232322222322444
11111111122222221616666332232322222322444
54444544442222221616666332232322222222444
11111111112222232161666633222222222222444
11111111112222232161666633222222222222444
44454444422222232161666633222222232222444
44454444422222232161666633222222232222444
11111111222322323216166863322222232224444
44544544223232323216168663322222322244444
11111111223232323216168663322222322444444
44545444422311231616668663322222322444444
5444544422316111166686633223222322244444
11111111223166766666686332323222322224444
11111111223167676668663323223232322222444
45444444223216766668666332322232322222444
44454444223231666666666332322232322222444
11111111223232116666663332322232322222444
11111111223232321111222332322232322222444
54454444422323232222233223332322223222222444
445444422232232222233323233232222222222244
11111112223222222233232332222222222222244
11111112223222222233223332222222222222224
```

MINI-LOOM SIZE
3" wide by 4" long (center opening)

BEADS
size 13° seed beads

CODE	COLOR	COUNT
1	smoke topaz trans	267
2	pale blue trans	803
3	cobalt (blue) trans	265
4	dark green trans	348
5	light green trans	46
6	Navajo white pearl	254
7	garnet trans	8
8	black opaque	41
9	topaz trans	48

THREAD

SIZE	COLOR	LENGTH
O	white	7 yards
B	white	6 yards

NEEDLES

#12 extra long
#13

16. Gotta Dance

```
11112211111111111111111111111111111111111
11122221111113331111113333111111111111111
11122221111113111311111311113111111111111
11422221111131111311113111113111111131111
11144422111131111311113111311111133111111
11114222221111333311111133311111331111111
11111422111111313333333133333331111111111
11111131113333111111111111111111111111111
11111113331111111115511111111111111111111
11111111111111111166511111111111111111111
11111111111111114446611111111111111111111
11111111111111114447441111111111111111111
11111111111111114444441111111111111111111
11111111111111114444441111177111111111111
11111111111111141444141117774111111111111
11111111111117477777747774711111111111111
11111111111117774777777444771111111111111
11111178277777774777477777711111111111111
11111178277777774447777777711111111111111
11111178277777777777777777711111111111111
11111178277777777777777777711111111111111
11111178277777777777777777711111111111111
11111178277777777777777772211111111111111
11111178277777777222222881111111111111111
11111178277722222288888771111111111111111
11111178222288888877777711111111111111111
11111178888877777799999911111111111111111
11111117777771999999999991111111111111111
11111111111119999999999911111111111111111
11111111111119999999966691111111111111111
11111111111119999999996691111111111111111
11111111111199999999116611111122141221111
11111111111111116611116611112222422221111
11111111111111116611166111122224222111111
11111111111111116666111111111124242421111
11111111111111111111111111111112444211111
11111111111111111111111111111122242221111
11111111111111111111111111111122242211111
11111111111111111111113333111134111111111
11111111113331111111311131113311111111111
11111111113111311111113333331111111111111
11111111111333333333331111111111111111111
11111113333311111111111111111111111111111
11133333111111111111111111111111111111111
```

CENTER

BEADS
size 11⁰ seed beads

CODE	COLOR	COUNT
1	yellow transparent	1256
2	orange trans	84
3	grey trans	93
4	black opaque matte	56
5	dark smoke topaz trans	3
6	white opal	23
7	aqua trans luster	167
8	garnet trans	28
9	capri trans	50

THREAD

SIZE	COLOR	LENGTH
O	white	5 yards
B	white	6 yards

NEEDLES

#12 extra long

MINI-LOOM SIZE
3" wide by 4" long (center opening)

```
11111111111111111122111111111113333333333333
11111111111111112221111111111113333333333333
11111111111111121111111111111113333333333333
11111111111111411111111111111113333333333333
11111111111141111111111111111113333333333333
11111111114111114444444444444444444333333
11111111141111115111111111111113333333333333
11111114111111111557666677776666333333333333
11111141111111111555766667777666688333333333333
11111141111111111175226666777766668888333333333333
11155111111111111766227666777766668833333333333
11555111111111111766667666777766668883333333333
15555111111111111766667666777766668883333333333
15551111111111117666666766677776666688333333333
11111111111111117666666766677776666688333333333
11111111111111117666666766677776666688333333333
11111111111111117666666766677776666688333333333
11111111111111117666666766677776666688333333333
11111111111111117666666766677776666688333333333
11111111111111117666664444444444444444443333    — CENTER
11111111114444476666567666777766668833333333
11111111115111176666655666777766668833333333
11111111111155117666665556667777666688333333
11111111111155517666666652267777666688333333
11111111111152276666666722677776666688333333
11111111111122766666667666777766668833333333
11111111111117666666766677776666688333333333
15511111111111176666667666777766668833333333
15555111111111117666667666777766668888333333
11555111111111117666667666777766668883333333
11155111111111117666667666777766668833333333
11111411111111117667666777766668883333333
11111141111111117667666777766668833333333
11111114111111117766677776666333333333333
11111111141111111111111111113333333333333
11111111141111444444444444444444433333
11111111141115111111111113333333333333
11111111111141115511111111113333333333333
11111111111112111555111111113333333333333
11111111111112221522111111113333333333333
11111111111111112122111111113333333333333
```

MINI-LOOM SIZE
3" wide by 4" long (center opening)

Note: If desired, "lace" drum by zig-zagging brown thread through topaz (#6) beads. Also "suspend" drum from supports on left and right using same color thread (see photo).

BEADS
size 11⁰ seed beads

CODE	COLOR	COUNT
1	light sapphire trans luster	692
2	dark smoke topaz trans	27
3	light green trans luster	323
4	dark topaz trans	76
5	white opal	48
6	topaz trans	301
7	light topaz trans luster	157
8	grey trans matte	56

THREAD

SIZE	COLOR	LENGTH
O	white	5 yards
B	white	6 yards
B	dark brown	1 yard

NEEDLES

#12 extra long
#13 (for lacing drum)

20. Kola

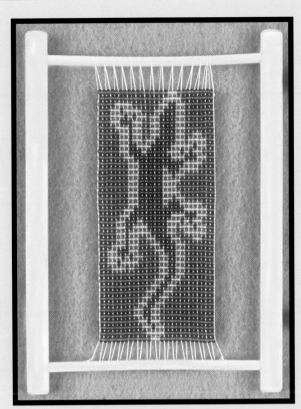

21. Little Lizzy

22. Many Honors

23. Medicine Wheel

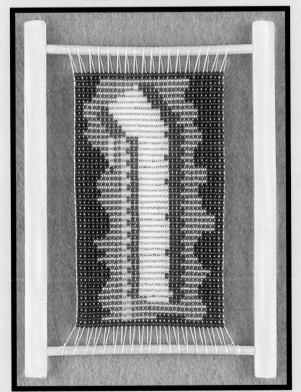

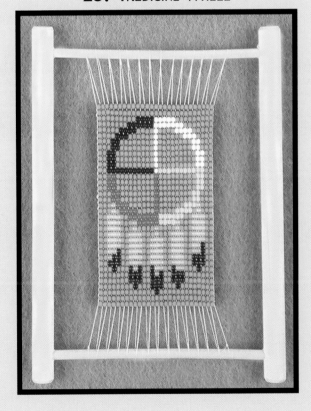

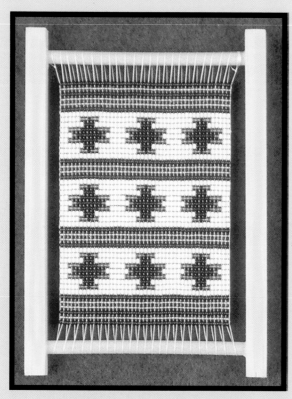

24. NAVAJO STYLE RUG: CHINLE

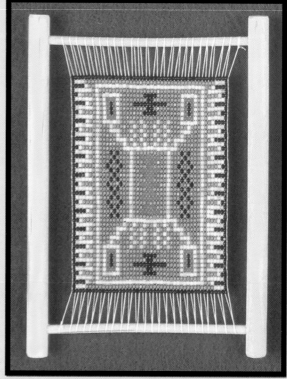

25. NAVAJO STYLE RUG: STORM PATTERN

26. NAVAJO STYLE RUG: TWO GREY HILLS

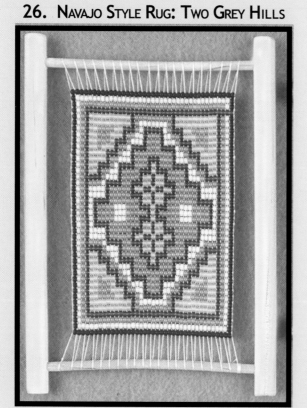

27. POWER OF PRAYER: EAGLE FEATHER

18. Jammin'

```
1111111111111111111111111122223333444
1111111111111111111111111222233334444
1111111111111111111111111112222333344445
1111111111111111111111111122223333444455
1111111111111111811111112222333344444555
1111111111181118118122223333444445555
1111111111118118118122223333444455556
1111111111111118181812222333344444555566
1111111111111118881222233334444555566
1111111118881888888823333444455556666
11111111888888888822233334444555566667
1111111888181118222333344445555666677
111111888118112822233334444555566666777
11111888111811228823333444455555666677777
1111888111188888833334444555566667777 1
111188811112222833344445555666677771 1
11118881112222383344445555666667777111
1111888112222333344445555666677771111
1111888122223333444455556666777711111
11118882222333344445555666677777111111
1111888222333344445558886677771111111
111188882333344445558866877771111111
11112888888888845555666678771111111111
11122288888884855556666888811111111111
11122238888844855556666888881111111111
1222233388844585566667788881111111111
22223333484455888666777788811111111111
2223333444855556666777788888811111111
22333344485555666677778888888811111111
23333444855556666777788888888811111111
3333444855556666777718888888888111111
333444888556666777711888888888811111
3344445555666677771118888888888111111
344445555666677771111888888888811111
4444555566667777111111888888881811111
44455556666777711111111188888818181111
44555566667777111111111181181181811 1
45555666677771111111111118118118181111
55556666777711111111111188188111811 1
55566667777111111111111111111111111111
556666777711111111111111111111111111111
```

CENTER —

MINI-LOOM SIZE
3" wide by 4" long (center opening)

BEADS
size 11° seed beads

CODE	COLOR	COUNT
1	light sapphire trans	575
2	garnet trans	95
3	hyacinth (orange) trans	116
4	citrine (yellow) trans	129
5	emerald trans	139
6	cobalt (blue) trans	129
7	deep amethyst trans	107
8	white opal	227

THREAD

SIZE	COLOR	LENGTH
O	white	5 yards
B	white	6 yards

NEEDLES

#12 extra long

```
1111111111111111111111111
1111111111111111111111111
1111111111111111111111111
1111111111111211111111111
1111111111121112111211111
1111111111121121121111111
1111111111112121211111111
1111111111111222111111111
1111111112221222222211111
1111111122222222211111111
1111111222121112111111111
1111111222112111211111111
1111122211121112111111111
1111222111122221111111111
1111222111111112111111111
1111222111111112111111111
1111222111111112111111111
1111222111111111111111111 ──CENTER
1111222111111111111111111
1111221111111111111111111
1111222111111111111111111
1111222111111111111111111
1111222211111111111111111
1111122222222211111111111
1111112222222121111111111
1111111222221211111111111
1111111122211121111111111
1111111112111122211111111
1111111111121111111111111
1111111111121111111111111
1111111112111111111111111
1111111121111111111111111
1111111211111111111111111
1111112221111111111111111
1111111111111111111111111
1111111111111111111111111
1111111111111111111111111
```

MINI-LOOM SIZE
3" wide by 4" long (center opening)

19. Kokopelli

50

20. KOLA

```
11111111111111111111111111111111111111111
11111122211111111131331141111111111111111
11111211121111111111131331441111111111111
11111211121111113333333333443333111111111
11111211121111111133334444333351111111111
12221112121111113333334444433555551111111
21112111111111133333334443334453555551111111
21112111111113333333444444444445551111111
21112111111133333333344554444444444455111111
12121111111133333335555444444444444445551111
11111111111133333355554444444444444551111
11111111133333333555544441444444444455111
11111111113333333555544441144444444444111
11111111333333335555544441111444434464111
11111333333333555555544441111114443436111
11111133333333555555544441111111144341111
11113333333335555555554444111111111111111
11111133333555555555554441111111111111111
11111133333445555555554441111111111111111
11111111444444455555554441111111111111111
11111111444444455555555554441111111111111111
11111114444444455555555554411111111111111111
11111114444444455555555555541111111111111111
11111444444444455555555555111111111111111111
11114444444444444455555555111111111111111111
11144444444444444455555551111111111111111
11444444444444444455555551111111111111111
14444445444444444455555551111111111111111
14444445444444444455555564441111111111111
44444445554444444555555564444441111111111
44444455554444444455556444444441111111111
44444455564444444444644444444441111111111
44444555555644444444444111111144411111111
44555555555566666644444441111114441111111
44555555555555555511111444111144411111111
44455555555555555511111144411114441111111111
44455555555555551111114441114441111111111
44444555555555511111114441174441111111111
44444555555541111114441177744111111111111
44444555556441111744441117771111111111111
44444555564441177744111711111111111111111
44444666644441177711111111111111111111111
44441666444441171111111111111111111111111
44411164444411111111111111111111111111111
44111114444411111111111111111111111111111
```

CENTER ←

BEADS
size 11° seed beads

CODE	COLOR	COUNT
1	peridot trans luster	874
2	gold supra (metallic)	22
3	black opaque matte	131
4	cinnamon opal matte	464
5	white opal	270
6	grey trans matte	23
7	topaz trans matte	16

THREAD

SIZE	COLOR	LENGTH
O	white	7 yards
B	white	6 yards

NEEDLES

#12 extra long
#13

MINI-LOOM SIZE
3" wide by 4" long (center opening)

```
11111111111111122111111111
11111111111111222211111111
11112222111111223322111111
11122322221112233322111111
11122232322122333322111111
11122333221122333322111111
11122232211223333221111111
11112232211223333221122111
11112232212233332212222111
11111223322233333222232211
11111223332333332223232111
11111122333333333222333221
11111112233333333333332111
11111112233333323333222111
11111112233333322323211111
11111112233333322221111111
11111112233333322111111111
11111112233333322221111111
11111112233333323232111111
11111112233333333332222111
11111122333333333333322211
11111223333333333322333221 — CENTER
11112333323333332223232111
11112233222333332212223221
11112232222233332211222221
11112232211223333221122111
11122232211122333322111111
11223332211112233322111111
11222323221111223322111111
11223222221111122333221111
11122221211111122332211111
11111111111111122332211111
11111111111112233221111111
11111111111223322111111111
11111111112233221111111111
11111111122332211111111111
11111111122332111111111111
11111111223322111111111111
11111111223322111111111111
11111111122332111111111111
11111111112232211111111111
11111111111222111111111111
11111111111221111111111111
```

MINI-LOOM SIZE
3" wide by 4" long (center opening)

BEADS
size 11° seed beads

CODE	COLOR	COUNT
1	dark brown trans matte	642
2	citrine (yellow) trans	301
3	dark kelly green trans	218

THREAD

SIZE	COLOR	LENGTH
O	white	4 yards
B	white	5 yards

NEEDLES

#12 extra long
#13

22. MANY HONORS EAGLE-FEATHER HEADDRESS

```
11111111111111111111111111111111111
11111222222222222222222221111111111
11111222222222344442222222221111111
11111222222233334444222222111111111
11112222223333333344442222211111111111
11222222233333333334444222222211111111
11222255333333333334442222222111111
11222555533333333333344442222211111
11122255555333333333334442222111111
11122255555333333333334444222111111
11222222555553333333334444222221111
11122222322655553333333344442222211111
11111222232266773333333344442222111111
11111122322655553333333344442221111111
11111112322667733333334444222111111
11111111322655533333333344442221111111
11111112422667733333334444222222111
11111122222655533333333444222221111
11111222222667733333334444222222211
11111222222655533333334444222111111
11111222222667733333334444222211111
11111222222655533333334444222211111
11111122222667733333334444222221111
11111122222655533333334444222221111
11111111222667733333344442222222211
11111111222655533333334444222222211
11111111222667733333334444222222211
11111111222655533333334444222211111
11112222222667733333334444222211111
11112222222655533333334444221111111
11111112222667733333334444222111111
11111222222655533333334444222111111
11111112222667733333334444222211111
11111111222655533333334444222222111
11111111222667733333334444222221111
11111111222655533333334444222211111
11111112222667733333334444222111111
11111122222655533333334444222111111
11111122222662222333334442222211111
11111122222662222222222222222221111
11111111222662222222222222222221111
11111122222662222221111111222211111
11111111111111111111111111111111111
```

CENTER

BEADS
size 11° seed beads

CODE	COLOR	COUNT
1	capri transparent	529
2	aqua trans luster	433
3	white opal	271
4	dark smoke topaz trans	138
5	garnet trans	60
6	topaz trans matte	48
7	grey trans matte	26

THREAD

SIZE	COLOR	LENGTH
O	white	5 yards
B	white	6 yards

NEEDLES
#12 extra long

MINI-LOOM SIZE
3" wide by 4" long (center opening)

```
1111111111111111111111111111
1111111111111111111111111111
1111111112222333331111111111
1111111222222333333311111111
1111122221111311113333111111
1111222111111311111133311111
1112211111111131111111133111
1112211111111311111111133111
1122111111111311111111113311
1122111111111131111111113311
1122111111111311111111113311
1122222222223444444444411
1155111111111511111111114411
1155111111111511111111114411
1155111111111511111111114411
1115511111111511111111144111
1115511111111511111111144111
1116555111111511111114446111
1116155551111151111444416111
1166611555555544444411166611
1166611165555544461111166611
1166611161111611116111166611
1166611666111611116661166611
1166611666116661166611166611
1166611666116661166611166711
1166711666116661166611166711
1166771166611666116661177711
1177711666116661166611177711
1117111767117661176611117111
1111111777117671177711111111
1111111777117771177711111111
1111111171117771171111111111
1111111111111711111111111111
1111111111111111111111111111
1111111111111111111111111111
```

— CENTER

MINI-LOOM SIZE
3" wide by 4" long (center opening)

23. MEDICINE WHEEL

BEADS
size 11° seed beads

CODE	COLOR	COUNT
1	blue turquoise opq matte	646
2	black opaque	38
3	white opaque	37
4	dark yellow opaque	38
5	red opaque	36
6	white opal (semi-trans)	107
7	dark smoke topaz trans	43

THREAD

SIZE	COLOR	LENGTH
O	white	4 yards
B	white	5 yards

NEEDLES

#12 extra long

NOTE: Use opaque beads for the background and wheel. The eagle feathers of transparent and semi-transparent beads will appear to glow when held up to the light.

24. NAVAJO STYLE RUG CHINLE

```
1111111111111111111111111111111111111111111111
2222222222222222222222222222222222222222222222
1111111111111111111111111111111111111111111111
2222222222222222222222222222222222222222222222
2222222222222222222222222222222222222222222222
1111111111111111111111111111111111111111111111
3333333333333333333333333333333333333333333333
3333344544333333333344544333333333344544433333
3333335553333333333335553333333333335553333333
3344455555444333344455555444333344455555544433
3334555555543333334555555554333333455555554333
3344455555444333344455555444333344455555544433
3333335553333333333335553333333333335553333333
3333344544333333333344544333333333344544433333
3333333333333333333333333333333333333333333333
1111111111111111111111111111111111111111111111
2222222222222222222222222222222222222222222222
2222222222222222222222222222222222222222222222
1111111111111111111111111111111111111111111111
3333333333333333333333333333333333333333333333
3333344544333333333344544333333333344544433333
3333335553333333333335553333333333335553333333
3344455555444333344455555444333344455555544433
3334555555543333334555555554333333455555554333
3344455555444333344455555444333344455555544433
3333335553333333333335553333333333335553333333
3333344544333333333344544333333333344544433333
3333333333333333333333333333333333333333333333
1111111111111111111111111111111111111111111111
2222222222222222222222222222222222222222222222
2222222222222222222222222222222222222222222222
1111111111111111111111111111111111111111111111
3333333333333333333333333333333333333333333333
3333344544333333333344544333333333344544433333
3333335553333333333335553333333333335553333333
3344455555444333344455555444333344455555544433
3334555555543333334555555554333333455555554333
3344455555444333344455555444333344455555544433
3333335553333333333335553333333333335553333333
3333344544333333333344544333333333344544433333
3333333333333333333333333333333333333333333333
1111111111111111111111111111111111111111111111
2222222222222222222222222222222222222222222222
2222222222222222222222222222222222222222222222
1111111111111111111111111111111111111111111111
2222222222222222222222222222222222222222222222
1111111111111111111111111111111111111111111111
```

CENTER +

BEADS
size 12° seed beads

CODE	COLOR	COUNT
1	smoke topaz trans	450
2	topaz trans	450
3	white opaque	792
4	light green trans	198
5	dark green trans	225

THREAD

SIZE	COLOR	LENGTH
O	white	7 yards
B	white	6 yards

NEEDLES

#12 extra long
#13

MINI-LOOM SIZE
3" wide by 4" long (center opening)

25. NAVAJO STYLE RUG STORM PATTERN

```
11111111111111111111111111111111111111111111111
12223333333333333333333333333333333333333332221
11112332222222222222222222222222222222223321111
12222232333333333333333333333333333333323222221
11233332322222333333311113333333322222323333211
12222232324442333333331133333333324442323222221
11112332324142333331111111111333324142323321111
12222232324142333333331133333333324142323222221
11233332324142333333331111333333324142323333211
12222232324442333333333333333333324442323222221
11112332322223332332333323323332222323321111
12222232333233333323323323323333332333323222221
11233332333222333233323333233323332223332 3333211
12222232333333233332332332332333323333323222221
11112332333332223323323332332322233333323321111
12222232333333323323323323323333333333323222221
11233332333333322222222222222222333333323333211
12222232333313133332333333333332333131333323222221
11112332333313333233444444332333313333323321111
12222232333313133323344443332333131333323222221
11233332333133313323333443333233133313332333211
12222232333131333323334444443323333131333323222221
11112332333313333233344443332333313333323321111
12222232333131333323334444433232333131333323222221
11233332331333133323444444333323313331332333211  CENTER
12222232333313133332334433332333131333323222221
11112332333313333233444433323333133333323321111
12222232333131333323344444433323331313333323222221
11233332333133313323334433332333133313332333211
12222232333131333323344443332333131333323222221
11112332333313333233444443332333313333323321111
12222232333131333323333333333233313133332323222221
11233332333333322222222222222222333333323333211
12222232333333323323233233233233333332322221
11112332333332223233233333233323222333323321111
12222232333333323333233233233233333323222221
11233332333222333233233333233323332223332333211
12222232333323333332332332332332333323232322221
11112332322223332332333323323332222323321111
12222232324442333333333333333333324442323222221
11233332324142333333331111333333324142323333211
12222232324142333333331133333333324142323222221
11112332324142333331111111111333324142323321111
12222232324442333333331133333333324442323222221
11233332322222333333311113333333322222323333211
12222232333333333333333333333333333333323222221
11112332222222222222222222222222222222223321111
12223333333333333333333333333333333333333332221
11111111111111111111111111111111111111111111111
```

MINI-LOOM SIZE
3" wide by 4" long (center opening)

BEADS
size 13° seed beads

CODE	COLOR	COUNT
1	black opaque	388
2	white opal	654
3	grey opaque	1110
4	red opaque	102

THREAD

SIZE	COLOR	LENGTH
O	white	7 yards
B	white	6 yards

NEEDLES

#13

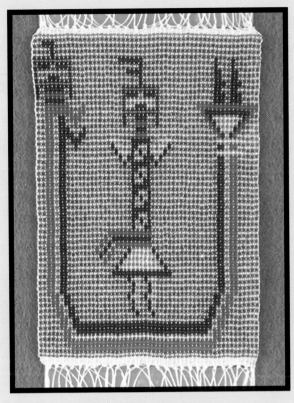

28. SAND PAINTING

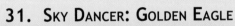

29. SISTER WOLF

30. SKY DANCER: BALD EAGLE

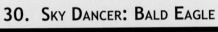

31. SKY DANCER: GOLDEN EAGLE

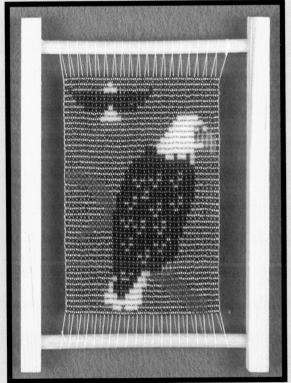

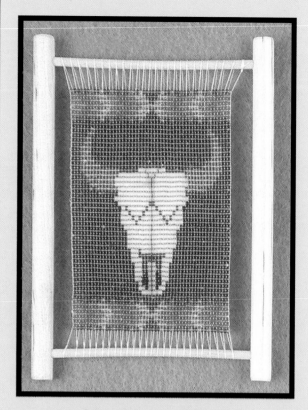

32. Tatanka Wakan

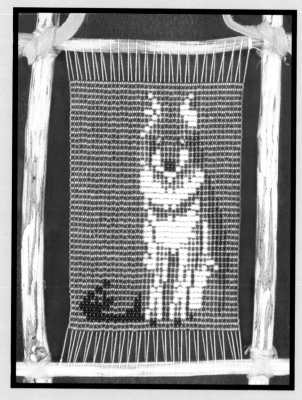

33. Song Dog

34. White Buffalo

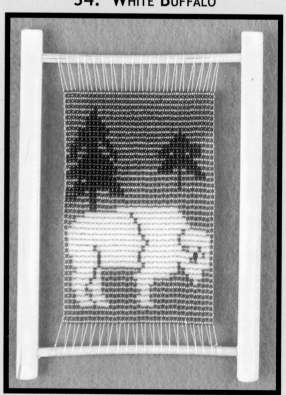

35. Yei Figures

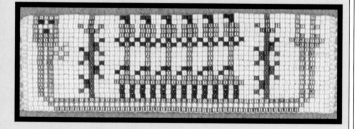

26. Navajo Style Rug
Two Grey Hills

```
1111111111111111111111111111111111111111
1222222222222222222222222222222222222221
1233333333333333333333333333333333333321
1234444444444444444444444444444444444444
1234555555555554333333333455555555554321
1234555555555554322222223455555555554321
1234553333554443244444234445533335554321
1234553333555433224333422334555333554321
1234553333544432224333422234445333554321
1234553555433244443334444233455535554321
1234555444322433333333422344455554321
1234555433222433344433342223345553334321
1234554443244443333454333444423444554321
1234554332243333444544433334223345554321
1234444322243333455455433334222344444321
1234333244443344455455444334444423334321
1234222243333334554454455433333342222431
1234222243333334445545544433333342222431
1234244443333333455455433333333444424321
1234243333222333444544433332223333424321
1234243333222333334544333332223333424321
1234243333222333444544433332223333424321
1234244443333333455455433333333444424321
1234222243333344455455444433333342222431
1234222243333334554454455433333342222431
1234333244443344455455444334444423334321
1234444322243333455455433334222344444321
1234554332243333444544433334223345554321
1234554443244443334543334444234445554321
1234555433222433344433342223345553334321
1234555444322433333333422344455554321
1234553555433244443334444233455535554321
1234553333554443244444234445533335554321
1234553333555433224333422334555333554321
1234553333544432244444234445533335554321
1234555555555554322222223455555555554321
1234555555555554333333333455555555554321
1234444444444444444444444444444444444321
1233333333333333333333333333333333333321
1222222222222222222222222222222222222221
1111111111111111111111111111111111111111
```

CENTER

BEADS
size 11° seed beads

CODE	COLOR	COUNT
1	black matte	155
2	Navajo white pearl	297
3	cinnamon opal matte	483
4	smoke topaz trans matte	419
5	topaz trans matte	245

THREAD

SIZE	COLOR	LENGTH
O	white	6 yards
B	white	5 yards

NEEDLES

#12 extra long
#13

MINI-LOOM SIZE
3" wide by 4" long (center opening)

```
11111111111111111111111111
11111111111131111111111111
11111111111222111111111111
11111111112222211111111111
11111111222222211111111111
11112111222222222111211111
11123211222222222211232111
11234321222222222212343211
12345432222222222223454321
23451543222222222234515432
34511154222522222245111543
45111115255562225511111154
51111111555565255111111115
11112111555565555511121111
11123211555565555511232111
11234321555565555512343211
12345432555535555523454321
23451543555565555534515432
34511154555535555545111543  —— CENTER
45111115555565555551111154
51111111555535555511111115
11112111155556555111121111
11123211115535511111232111
11234321112777211112343211
12345432123777321234543211
23451543234777432345154321
34511154345777543451115432
45111115451777154511111154
51111111511777115111111115
11111111111777111111111111
11111111117171711111111111
11111111171711711111111111
11117111717117111111111111
11111711717171711111111111
11111177111717111111111111
11111111117111777111111111
11111177711111117111111111
11111111111111111111111111
```

MINI-LOOM SIZE
3" wide by 4" long (center opening)

27. POWER OF PRAYER
EAGLE FEATHER

BEADS
size 11° seed beads

CODE	COLOR	COUNT
1	aqua trans luster	515
2	black opaque	127
3	garnet trans	59
4	citrine (yellow) trans	54
5	white opal	140
6	grey trans luster	8
7	dark smoke topaz trans	47

THREAD

SIZE	COLOR	LENGTH
O	white	4 yards
B	white	5 yards

NEEDLES

#12 extra long

28. SAND PAINTING

```
1111111111111111111111111111111111111111111111111111111
1122211111111111111111111111111111111111111111111111111
1111211111111111111111111111111111111111111111111111111
1111211111111111111111111111111111111111111111111111111
3333333311111111111122222211111111111111111611161111111
3222122231111111111111121111111111111111111161116111111
3111111131111111111111122221111111111111111166116611111
3112221131111111111111112111111111111111111166116611111
3333333311111111111111111211111111111111111166616661111
6166666161111111111111133333333111111111111166116611111
6144444161111111111111132225222311111111111166616661111
1166666111111111111111135555555311111111111166616661111
1144444411114111111111135522255311111111144444444444444
1144444441144111111111133333333311111111146666666666641
1144566144411111111111161116661161111111114655555556411
1144566114111111111111161144411611111111111465555564115
1144566611611111111111166611111111111111111146555641151
1144566616611111111111144411111111111111111114656411515
1144566166611111115511166666111551111111111115555555151
1144566116111111116551566556651556111111111116654411511
1144566111111111116555656565556111111111111115555555111
1144566111111111116566556665611111111111111116654411111
1144566111111111111616666616111111111111111116654411111
1144566111111111111166556111111111111111111116654411111
1144566111111111111116565611111111111111111116654411111
1144566111111111111116556611111111111111111116654411111
1144566111111111111116666611111111111111111116654411111
1144566111111111111116655611111111111111111116654411111
1144566111111111111116565611111111111111111116654411111
1144566111111111111116556611111111111111111116654411111
1144566111111111111116666611111111111111111116654411111
1144566111111111111116655611111111111111111116654411111
1144566111111111111116565611111111111111111116654411111
1144566111111111111116556611111111111111111116654411111
1144566111111114444444444411111111111111111116654411111
1144566111111114166666666661111111111111111116654411111
1144566111111114161444444441111111111111111116654411111
1144566111111416141116555556111111111111111116654411111
1144566111111614111655555556111111111111111116654411111
1144566111111141116555555556111111111111111116654411111
1144566111111111165555555555611111111111111116654411111
1144566111111111166666666666666111111111111116654411111
1144566111111111111665516551111111111111111116654411111
1144566111111111111111651116511111111111111116654411111
1144566111111111111111651116511111111111111116654411111
1114456611111111111111655165511111111111111166544111111
1114456611111111111111651116511111111111111166544111111
1111445661111111111111651116511111111111166544111111111
1111445661111111111111161116111111111111116654411111111
1111114456611111111111116111611111111111116654411111111
1111114456666666666666666666666666666666665441111111111
1111114456666666666666666666666666666666665441111111111
1111114455555555555555555555555555555555554411111111111
1111111444444444444444444444444444444444441111111111111
1111111114444444444444444444444444444444441111111111111
1111111111111111111111111111111111111111111111111111111
```

CENTER

BEADS

size 14° seed beads

CODE	COLOR	COUNT
1	topaz trans rainbow	1996
2	black opaque	36
3	dark topaz trans	48
4	garnet trans	298
5	crystal aurora borealis	243
6	cobalt (blue) trans	403

THREAD

SIZE	COLOR	LENGTH
O	white	6 yards
B	white	8 yards

NEEDLES

#13 (if using Japanese beads)
#15 (if using Czech beads)

MINI-LOOM SIZE
3" wide by 4" long (center opening)
3" wide by 6 1/2" long if removing finished piece from loom

29. SISTER WOLF

```
111111111122211111111111111111221111111
111111111233321111111111111122332111111
111111112344332211111111111233443211111
111111112344433321111111111233444321111
111111123443443332221112223344343211111
111111123433443333322233333443444321111
111111123433443333333333333334434432111
111111234434433333333333333334434432111
111111234434333333333333333334444321111
111111234433333333333333333333434321111
111111234333333333333333333333333332111
111111233333333334433333443333333332111
111111233333333334443334443333333332111
111111233333335534333433553333333332111
111112333333333535364346355333333332111
111112333333333366434663333333332111
111123333333333666444667333348333321
11123333333333366444446644334883333211
1123333344333387869996678844888333321
1123333888444888699999788888888333321
1233333888888838889998883888888333321
1233333888888838844483388878833333321
1233333338878888833333888787833333321
1233333338788888833888888878333333321
1233333337887888888888887887333333211
1233333338878887888888787888333333211
1233333338788887888888887888333333211
1233333333888887887888787888333333211
1233333333333888788878838333333332111
123233333333333887887878333333333321111
1122333333333338888878883333333333321111
111233333333333388787833333333332211111
111123233333333338878833333333321111111
111121233333333338887333333333321111111
111111233333333338883333333333211111111
1111112333333333333333333333333211111111
1111112332323333333333333333322111111111
1111112322333333333333333323211111111111
1111112121233333333333333212111111111111
11111111123333333333333321111111111111111
111111111123333333333221111111111111111
11111111111233333332111111111111111111
1111111111111222333211111111111111111
111111111111111123321111111111111111
111111111111111112211111111111111111
```

— CENTER

MINI-LOOM SIZE
3" wide by 4" long (center opening)

BEADS
size 11° seed beads

CODE	COLOR	COUNT
1	bottle green trans matte	567
2	peridot trans luster	124
3	black matte	669
4	grey trans matte	88
5	dk topaz trans luster	8
6	topaz trans matte	19
7	lt topaz trans matte	35
8	white opal AB matte	189
9	black opaque	11

THREAD

SIZE	COLOR	LENGTH
O	white	7 yards
B	white	6 yards

NEEDLES

#12 extra long
#13

30. Sky Dancer
Bald Eagle

```
11111111111111111111111111111111111111111
11111111111211111111111111111111111111111
13111111111222111111111311111111111111111
11333333333333333333331111111111111111111
11133333333333333333331111111111111111111
11111333333233333331111111111111111111111
11111111112221111111111111111111111111111
11111111122222111111111111112222211111111
11111111111111111111111111122222221111111
111111111111111111111111111222222X62111
11111111111111111111111111112222222666511
11111111111111111111111111122222222555551
11111111111111111111111112222222222225551
11111111111111111111111333222222222111151
11111111111111111111133333322322321111111
11111111111111111113333333333333321111111
11111111111111111133333333333333331111111
77777111111111111333333333433334333111111
77777777111111111334343434334343333111111
11177777777111113333433343333343333111111
11111177777111133333343333333333331111111
11111177777113333434443333334343331111111
11111111177777733434333334343434331111111
11111111117777333433334343333433311111111
11111111111773333333333343333333311111111
11111117777733343433433334333311111111111
11111177777733334343433434343333111111111
11117771111133333343333343333311111111111
11117711111113333433333333433111111111111
11111111111133434333334343333111111111111
11111111111133343333343343333111111111111
11111111111133333343433333311111111111111
11111111111133333334333331111111111111111
11111111111133333333333333555111111111111
11111111111133434332277575777111111111111
11111111111123443322117777777111111111111
11111111111123333322111177777711111111111
11111111111123333222111111777777111111111
11111111111122233222211111117777777711111
11111111111122222222211111111111777777111
11111111111112212221111111111111177777111
11111111111111111111111111111111117777111
```

CENTER ◄

BEADS
size 11° seed beads

CODE	COLOR	COUNT
1	light sapphire trans luster	972
2	white opal	107
3	dark smoke topaz trans	344
4	dark topaz trans luster	53
5	citrine (yellow) trans	14
6	grey transparent	4
7	cinnamon opal matte	101
X	2mm tiger eye bead (drilled)	1

THREAD

SIZE	COLOR	LENGTH
O	white	5 yards
B	white	6 yards

NEEDLES

#12 extra long

MINI-LOOM SIZE
3" wide by 4" long (center opening)

```
11111111111111111111111111111111111111111
1111111111111212122121211111111111111111112
1111111111112122222222222121111111111111112
11111111111122222777777772222211111111111212
111111111211117777777777772211111111111111222
1111111112222277777775222222111111111111223
11111111122277777775722111111111111111111233
11111112122777777775772222111111111111111233
111111122266667775777522111111111111112333
11111122266566777577775211111111111111122333
111112226366566675777752221111111111122333
1121222333636766657775552212112111111123333
1121223333773376577355552222121121212123333
1122233335337336573355555522212212122333333
1122233335733736533355555552222222222233333
11223333357773765333335555522222223333333
12223333553737335333333335555553333333333
12233333537333735333333333333553333333333
12233335537777336333333333333333333333333
12233335566677336333333333333333333333333
12333335533363736333333333333333333333433333
1233333533333673633333333333333334333343333
123333353443336535553333333333333334333334333
1233333534433365555533333333333333343333343
123333353333336555553333333333343333343333333
12333335633366535533333333333334333333333333
12333335566655535333333333333343343333333
123333355555353533333333333333343343333333
12333335553333333333333333343334333334333333
12333335533333333333333333334333343333334333
12333335333333333333333333333343333434343333
123333333333333333333334333333333333433333
11233333333333333333333334333333343333343333
1123333333333333333333333343333334333333333
11233333333333333333333334334334333333333
1123233333333333333333333333334333343343333
11222333333333334333343343333334333333343333
11222323333333333343334343433333343333334333
11122222333333333343333433433333333333333433
1111212123333333333334333433343333333333333
1111212122333333333333333333333333334333333
11111112223233333333333333333334333433333
1111111212222333333333334333333333433343333
11111111111212233333333334333433333433334333
1111111111112122222323333334333433334333333
11111111111111121222222232233323344333333
111111111111111111221222222322333333433333
1111111111111111111211221222222222334333
1111111111111111111111121112221222222334333
111111111111111111111111112112212222233333
1111111111111111111111111111211212222333
11111111111111111111111111111111111222223
1111111111111111111111111111111111211222
111111111111111111111111111111111111111111
```

— CENTER (aligned with the row near the middle of the grid)

31. SKY DANCER
GOLDEN EAGLE

BEADS
size 14º seed beads

CODE	COLOR	COUNT
1	cobalt (blue) trans	638
2	sky blue opaque	274
3	dark topaz trans	1033
4	black opaque	77
5	black opaque matte	101
6	lt topaz trans luster	38
7	grey trans luster	94

THREAD

SIZE	COLOR	LENGTH
O	white	5 yards
B	white	6 yards

NEEDLES

#13 (if using Japanese beads)
#15 (if using Czech beads)

MINI-LOOM SIZE

3" wide by 4" long (center opening)

32. Tatanka Wakan

Note: The black thread is used to represent the joining of the skull plates. Wrap it around pairs of weft threads, one row at a time, and use a small amount of fabric glue at the top and bottom to hold it in place. Use the picture on page 58 to place the thread.

CENTER →

BEADS
size 13⁰ true cuts (Charlottes)

CODE	COLOR	COUNT
1	aqua trans luster	1514
2	yellow trans	140
3	orange trans	264
4	garnet trans	136
5	topaz trans	146
6	white opal	343
7	grey trans	41
8	black opaque	16

THREAD

SIZE	COLOR	LENGTH
O	white	6 yards
B	white	7 yards
B	black	1 yard

NEEDLES

#12 extra long
#13

```
31141131121131141131121111112113114113112113114113
33444333222333444333222111122233344433322233344433
33344433322223334443333222211222333444333222333444333
23334443332222333444333322222223334443332223334443332
33344433322233344433322221122233344433322233344433
33444333222333444333222111122233344433322233344433
31141131121131141131121111112113114113112113114113
11111111111111111111111111111111111111111111111111
11111151111111111111111111111111111111111151111111
11111155111111111111111111111111111111111115511111
11111551111111111111111111111111111111111111551111
11111551111111111111111111111111111111111111551111
11155511111111111111111111111111111111111111555111
11155511111111111111111111111111111111111111555111
11155551111111111111111111111111111111111111555111
11155555111111111111111111111111111111111115555111
11155555551111111111111111111111111111111555555111
11155555555555551111116666666611111555555555555111
11115555555555556666666666666666666555555555551111
11111555555555556666666666666666666665555555551111
11111155555555566666666666666666666666555555511111
11111115555555566666666666666666666666555555511111
11111111555555566666666666666666666665555555511111
11111111111111116666666666666666666661111111111111
11111111111111116666666666666666666661111111111111
11111111111111118666666666776666666681111111111111
11111111111111118676666676676666667681111111111111
11111111111111116676666766667666766611111111111111
11111111111111116666767666666767666611111111111111
11111111111111116666766666667666661111111111111111
11111111111111111666666666666666611111111111111111
11111111111111111666666666666666611111111111111111
11111111111111111666666666666666611111111111111111
11111111111111111666666666666666611111111111111111
11111111111111111166766666666661111111111111111111
11111111111111111166777777776611111111111111111111
11111111111111111166677777766611111111111111111111
11111111111111111166776677661111111111111111111111
11111111111111111166776677661111111111111111111111
11111111111111111166786687661111111111111111111111
11111111111111111668866886611111111111111111111111
11111111111111111688668886111111111111111111111111
11111111111111111668668866111111111111111111111111
11111111111111111666666611111111111111111111111111
11111111111111111111111111111111111111111111111111
31141131121131141131121111112113114113112113114113
33444333222333444333222111122233344433322233344433
33344433322223334443333222221222333444333222333444333
23334443332222333444333322222223334443332223334443332
33344433322233344433322221122233344433322233344433
33444333222333444333222111122233344433322233344433
31141131121131141131121111112113114113112113114113
```

MINI-LOOM SIZE
3" wide by 4" long (center opening)

33. Song Dog

```
1111111111111111111111111111111111111111111111
1111111111111111113311111111133111111111111
1111111111111111135731111111137531111111111
1111111111111111134473111111137553111111111
1111111111111111134477311137774531111111111
1111111111111111137757344437777311111111111
1111111111111111133722444227773111111111111
1111111111111111137234444432773111111111111
1111111111111111172334444433231111111111111
1111111111111111172322444442235511111111111
1111111111111111123355x54445x55551111111111
1111111111111111122555334335555551111111111
1111111111111111122557333337735551111111111
1111111111111111172522366637335551111111111
1111111111111111172577666735322511111111111
1111111111111111177725577755222775111111111
1111111111111111177722257522727775511111111
1111111111111111177777225222777753511111111
1111111111111111177777272727777553551111111
1111111111111111177777777773555355111111111
1111111111111111157777777355575355511111111
1111111111111111173533757355377535555111111
1111111111111111137355535553775533555551111
1111111111111111137733373777773355555111111
1111111111111111173777777777733755555111111
1111111111111111177377777777733572555551111
1111111111111111177377777777725725555111111
1111111111111111177377777772225725555511111
1111111111111111157722777722225725555511111
1111111111111111157722257577222572555551111
1111111111111111175722255577225222555555111
1111111111111111177722755577225227755555111
1111111111111111137722753372225275515555111
1111111111111111133322753372757777455511111
1111111111111111133372753372757777444551111
1111111116644444444332725337277577744355111
1111116644444444443372753327757777443335111
1111166446444444463377753377757777443335111
1116646466644444663372753372757777443355111
1166666666644444663372753722757777443355111
1116666644444666663722557227533344433511111
1111666666666666667337557337563334431111111
1111111111111111111366311366311111111111111
1111111111111111111111111111111111111111111
```

← CENTER

MINI-LOOM SIZE
3" wide by 4" long (center opening)

BEADS		
size 11° seed beads		

CODE	COLOR	COUNT
1	peridot transparent	1018
2	light topaz transparent	103
3	topaz transparent	145
4	dark topaz trans luster	95
5	grey transparent	179
6	black opaque	61
7	white opal	245
X	2mm tiger eye bd (drilled)	2

THREAD

SIZE	COLOR	LENGTH
O	white	7 yards
B	white	6 yards

NEEDLES

#12 extra long

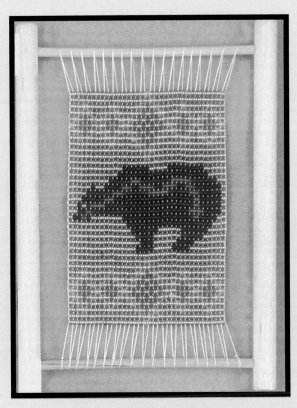

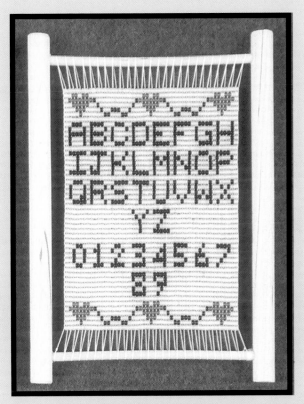

36. Zuni Bear Fetish   **37.** Old Fashioned Sampler

38. Loving Hearts   **39.** Just For Fun Dolphin

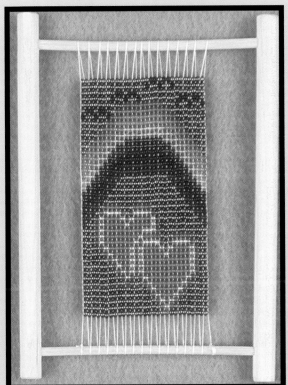

42. Orca Joy: Yes!!

40. Orca Joy: Do-Wet

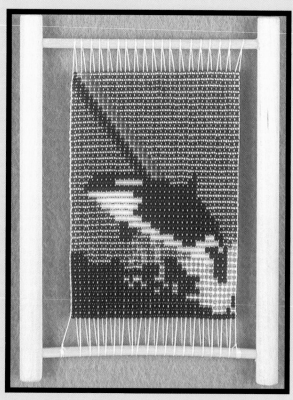

41. Orca Joy: Jump Left

43. Under The Sea

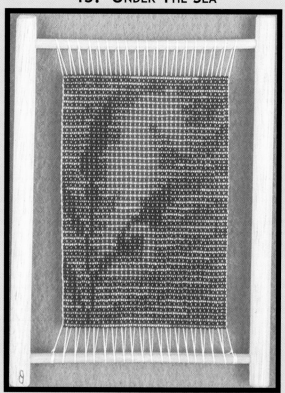

44. U.S.A.

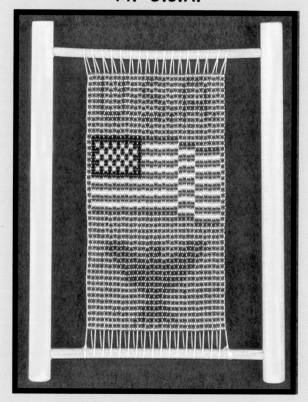

34. WHITE BUFFALO

```
1111111111111111111111111111111111111111
1111111111111111111111111111111111111111
1111111111111111111111111111111111111111
1111111211111111111111111111111111111111
1111112211111111111111111111111111111111
1111122221111111111111111111111111111111
1111122222111111111111111111111111111111
1112222222211111111111111111211111111111
1112222222211111111111111112221111133
1122222212211111111111111122222113333
1222122221122111111111111112222222222333
1221122221122111111111122212221222333
2221222222212111111111111222222233333
1112222222221111111111332222422223333
1222222222222221111113333222343222333
2222222222221111333333333334333322233
1112122222221113333333333333433333333
1122222222222233333333333333433333333
2222214433322223333333333333333333333
2221114433333333333333333333333333333
1113334433333333333333333333333333333
1133334433333333555555555555555333333333
1333355555555555655555555555553333333
3335555555555555556555555555553333333
3355555555555555556555555555555333333
3555555555555555556555555555575555533
5555555555555555556555555557555555553
5555555555555555555655555557555555553
5555555655555555556555555555577556553
5555555655555555556555555555555x5653
3355555655555555556555555555555665553
3355555655555555556555555555655555553
3335556533333333365555555555665555633
3355555653333333355555555533336555333
3355556553333333355553333333333653333
3335553553333333355533333333333333333
3335533553333333355333333333333333333
3335553553333333355333333333333333333
3333555353333333355333333333333333333
3333333333333333333333333333333333333
3333333333333333333333333333333333333
3333333333333333333333333333333333333
```

CENTER —

MINI-LOOM SIZE
3" wide by 4" long (center opening)

BEADS
size 11° seed beads

CODE	COLOR	COUNT
1	light sapphire trans luster	410
2	dark green trans	182
3	peridot trans	523
4	dark brown trans matte	13
5	white opal	392
6	grey trans	28
7	dark topaz trans luster	5
X	2 mm black onyx bead (drilled)	1

THREAD

SIZE	COLOR	LENGTH
O	white	5 yards
B	white	6 yards

NEEDLES

#12 extra long

```
11111111111111111111
11111211111111111111
11313221111111111111
33333222222222222111
11111222444444444211
11313222333333333421
33333221111111111342
11111211111111111342
11111111111111111342
11111111111111111342
11511611716117111342
11151167111671111342
55557777777777777342
11151111671111671342
11511161171161171342
11111111111111111342
11111111111111111342
11111811111119111342
11999181111199888342
88999899999899911342
81999181111819988342
11111811111181911342
11999181111199888342
88999899999899911342
81999181111819988342
11111811111181911342
11999181111199888342
88999899999899911342
81999181111819988342
11111811111181911342  ── CENTER
11999181111199888342
88999899999899911342
81999181111819988342
11111811111181911342
11999181111199888342
88999899999899911342
81999181111819988342
11111811111181911342
11999181111199888342
88999899999899911342
81999181111819988342
11111811111181911342
11111111111111111342
11111111111111111342
11511611716117111342
11151167111671111342
55557777777777777342
11151111671111671342
11511161171161171342
11111111111111111342
11111111111111111342
11111121311111111342
11111112131111111342
33333321311111111342
38443223333333333421
34483224444444444211
38443222222222222111
33333311111111111111
11111111111111111111
```

BEADS
Japanese Delica beads

CODE	COLOR	COUNT
1	cream opaque	652
2	red opaque	97
3	blue opaque	104
4	crystal AB	77
5	green iris	16
6	blue iris	16
7	green matte	44
8	black opaque	100
9	red metallic	133

THREAD

SIZE	COLOR	LENGTH
O	white	4 yards
B	white	4 yards

NEEDLES

#12 extra long
#13

MINI-LOOM SIZE

3" wide by 7" long (center opening)

36. Zuni Bear Fetish

```
11111111111111111311111111111111111
11111111111111131311111111111111111
11131111131111131413111113111113111
11313111313111131413111131311131311
13141313141313141514131314131314131
31444131444131415151413144413144413
13141313141313141514131314131314131
11313111313111131413111131311131311
11131111131111131413111113111113111
11111111111111131311111111111111111
11111111111111113111111111111111111
11111111111111111111111111111111111
1111111111122222211112222222211111
1111111111122222222222222222221111
11111111112222552222222555522222211
11111211222255225555225552255222221
11112222225522222225555222225522221
11122222552222222222222222225222221
11212555522222222222222222225222221
11225222222222222222222222255522221
12252111111122222222222222225222211
11111111111112222222222222222222111
11111111111112222221111122222221111
11111111111112222111111222221111111
11111111111112221111122221111111111
11111111111112222111222211111111111
11111111111111111111111111111111111
11111111111111131111111111111111111
11111111111111131311111111111111111
11131111131111131413111113111113111
11313111313111131413111131311131311
13141313141313141514131314131314131
31444131444131415151413144413144413
13141313141313141514131314131314131
11313111313111131413111131311131311
11131111131111131413111113111113111
11111111111111131311111111111111111
11111111111111131111111111111111111
```

CENTER

MINI-LOOM SIZE
3" wide by 4" long (center opening)

BEADS
size 11° seed beads

CODE	COLOR	COUNT
1	aqua trans luster	841
2	black opaque	252
3	citrine (yellow) trans	128
4	hyacinth (orange) trans	64
5	garnet trans	45

THREAD

SIZE	COLOR	LENGTH
O	white	5 yards
B	white	6 yards

NEEDLES

#12 extra long

```
111111111111111111111111111111111111111111111111
112212221111111111111122122111111111111112212211
122222223111111111113222222231111111111322222221
112222211311111111131122222113111111111311222221
111222111311333113111122211113113331131111222111
111121111113311133111111211111113311133111112111
111111111111111111111111111111111111111111111111
114441144441114441144441144444144444114441411141
141114141114141114141114141111141111141111411141
144444144441141111114111141444411144411141144144441
141114141114141114141114141111141111141114141111
141114144441114441144441144444141111114441411141
111111111111111111111111111111111111111111111111
144444144444141114141111141114141114144411444411
111411111411141141141111144144141141411141411141
111411111411144411141111141414141414141114144411
111411141141114114141111141114141144141114141111
144444144441141114144444141114141114144411411111
111111111111111111111111111111111111111111111111
114441144441114444144444141114141114141114141141
141114141114141111114111411141114141114141141411
141114144441114441111141114111414114141141141114111
141144141141111114111411141114141141141441441141411
114444141114144441114111114441114111141114141411141
111111111111111111111111111111111111111111111111
111111111111111111141114144444111111111111111111
111111111111111111141411111411111111111111111111
111111111111111111141111141111111111111111111111
111111111111111111141114111111111111111111111111
111111111111111111141144444111111111111111111111
111111111111111111111111111111111111111111111111
111111111111111111111111111111111111111111111111
111441111411114411144441111141144441114111444411
114114114411141141111411114411411111411111111411
114114114111114111144111141414144411144411111114111
114114114111114111111141144441111141141141141111
111441114441144441144441111141144441144441411111
111111111111111111111111111111111111111111111111
111111111111111444411444411111111111111111111111
111111111111111141141141141111111111111111111111
111111111111111111144111114441111111111111111111
111111111111111111141411111411111111111111111111
111111111111111111144441114111111111111111111111
111111111111111111111111111111111111111111111111
112212221111111111111122122111111111111112212211
122222223111111111113222222231111111111322222221
112222211311111111131122222113111111111311222221
111222111311333113111122211113113331131111222111
111121111113311133111111211111113311133111112111
111111111111111111111111111111111111111111111111
```

— CENTER

37. Old Fashioned Sampler

MINI-LOOM SIZE
3" wide by 4" long (center opening)

BEADS
size 13° seed beads

CODE	COLOR	COUNT
1	white opal	1857
2	garnet trans	120
3	kelly green trans	52
4	cobalt (blue) trans	421

THREAD

SIZE	COLOR	LENGTH
O	white	7 yards
B	white	6 yards

NEEDLES

#12 extra long
#13

38. LOVING HEARTS

```
111111111111111116616611111111
111111111111111161161161111111
111111166166111111111111111111
111111161161161111111111661661
111111111122222222211161161116
166166112222222222222211111111
611611622233333333332221111111
111111223333333333333322111111
111112233344444444433322111111
111122334444444444444433221111
111223344455555555544443322111
112233445555555555555544332211
122334455566666666665554433221
223344556666666666666655443322
233445566677777777766655544332
334455667777777777777766554433
344556677111111111111776655443
445566771111111111111177665544
455667711111111111111117766554
556677111111111111111111776655   ← CENTER
566771111111111111111111177665
667712222111122221111111117766
677128888212888821111111111776
771282222282822228211111111177
711282222282222228211111111117
111282222222288821111111111111
111282222222282222111122221111
111282222222282888821288882111
111128222228282222282822228211
111112822228282222282222228211
111111282228282222222222228211
111111128228282222222222228211
111111112828282222222222228211
111111111282128222222222282111
111111111121112822222222821111
111111111111112822222821111111
111111111111111128222282111111
111111111111111112828211111111
111111111111111111128211111111
111111111111111111112111111111
```

BEADS
size 11° seed beads

CODE	COLOR	COUNT
1	light sapphire trans luster	522
2	garnet trans	256
3	hyacinth (orange) trans	58
4	citrine (yellow) trans	58
5	emerald trans	58
6	cobalt (blue) trans	86
7	dark amethyst trans	56
8	crystal aurora borealis (AB)	66

THREAD

SIZE	COLOR	LENGTH
O	white	4 yards
B	white	5 yards

NEEDLES

#12 extra long

MINI-LOOM SIZE
3" wide by 4" long (center opening)

```
32111111111111111111111111
43211111111111111111111111
54321111111111111111111111
65432111111111111111111111
76543211111111111111111111
17654321111111111111111111
11765432111111111111111111
11176543211111111111111111
11117654321111111111111111
11111765432111111111111111
11111176543211111111111111
11111117654321111111111111
11111111888832111111111111
11111111888882111111111111
11111111888888888111111111
11111111888888888888111111
11111118888888888888888111
11111188888888888832111111  — CENTER
11111888888111178543211111
11111888811111187654321111
11111888111111117765432111
11111881111111111176543211
11118118111111111117654321
11181111811111111111765432
11111111111111111111176543
11111111111111111111117654
11111111111111111111111765
11111111111111111111111176
11119911111991111199111117
11199191111991911199191119
11659111156911115651111166
16665611666661165666611666
66666666666666666666666656
65666666666566655666666566
66665566666666666566666656
```

MINI-LOOM SIZE
3" wide by 4" long (center opening)

39. JUST FOR FUN
DOLPHIN

BEADS
size 11° seed beads

CODE	COLOR	COUNT
1	light sapphire trans luster	561
2	garnet trans	21
3	hyacinth (orange) trans	21
4	citrine (yellow) trans	19
5	emerald trans	35
6	cobalt (blue) trans	104
7	dark amethyst trans	19
8	black diamond trans luster	77
9	crystal aurora borealis (AB)	18

THREAD

SIZE	COLOR	LENGTH
O	white	4 yards
B	white	5 yards

NEEDLES

#12 extra long
#13

40. ORCA JOY
DO-WET

```
11111111111111111111111111111111112345
11111111111111111111111111111111123456
11111111111111111111111111111111234567
11111111111111111111111111111112345671
11111111111111111111111111111123456711
11111111111111111111111111111234567111
11111111111111111111111111112345671111
11111111111111111111111111123456711111
11111111111111111111111111234567111111
11111111111111111111111112345671111111
11111111111111111111111123456711111111
11111111111111111111112345671111111111
11111111111111111111123456711111111111
11111111111111111112345671111111111111
11111111111111111123456711111111111111
11111111111111111888567111111111111111
11111111111111111288887111111111111111
11111111111111112348888888888888111111
11111111111111123888888888888888881111
11111111111111123888888888888999988811
1111111110111028888888888888888888881
11110111110000888888888888889999999991
11011110100008888888888888899999999911
11111010000088889999988881888811111111
66111100000888988999988811888811111166
66600000008889899991111111188811116666
66666600000888889088881111111111166666
66600000000888800008888111111166666666
60000000000880000008888888888888666666
66600000000000000008888888888888886666
66666600000066668888888888889999988866
66600000006666088888888888888888888886
60066666666668888888888888889999999996
66666666060608888888888888899999999966
66666606666888899999888868888666666666
60006666000888988999888668888866666666
66600000000888889000006666666666666666
66660000000888800000666666666666666666
60000000000880000000066666666666666666
66600000000000000066666666666666666666
```

CENTER

MINI-LOOM SIZE
3" wide by 4" long (center opening)

BEADS
size 11° seed beads

CODE	COLOR	COUNT
1	light sapphire trans luster	674
2	garnet trans	20
3	hyacinth (orange) trans	18
4	citrine (yellow) trans	16
5	emerald trans	16
6	cobalt (blue) trans	220
7	deep amethyst trans	15
8	black matte	277
9	white opal	71
0	crystal aurora borealis (AB)	153

THREAD

SIZE	COLOR	LENGTH
O	white	5 yards
B	white	6 yards

NEEDLES

#12 extra long

```
54321111111111111111111111111110000000
6543211111111111111111111110000000000000
76543211111111111111111111110000000000000
17654321111111111111111110000000000000000
11765432111111111100000000000000000000000
1111765432111111111110000000000000000
11111765432111111111111111000000000000000
111111765432111111111111111110000000000
1111111765432111111111111111111111100000
11111117654321111111111111111111111111111
111111117654321111111111111111111111111
1111111117654321111111111111111111111111
11111111117654321111111111111111111111111
111111111117654321111111111111111111111
1111111111117654321111111111111111111111
11111111111117654321111111111111111111111
111111111111117654321111111111111111111
11111888888888865432111111811111111111
1111188888899999988888811118811111111111
11188888888888888888888888111111111111
1111999999999988888888888888111111111111
1111119999999999888888888888811111111111
11111199999999988888888888888811111111111
1111111119999988888888888888888811111111
1111111111199999988888888888888811111111
111111111118899999888888888888881111
1111111111188811999998888888888881111
1111111111188811119999988888889988111
1111111111111101101199998889999981110
1111111111111101101111199999988898800
66611111111111010110111111199998888800
666611111166110110110166600000009988800
66666666666611106666066660000000088800
6666666666666666666066666000000088800
666666666666060066600666666600008800
6666666666666060666606066660000000000
6666666666666666666066606666600000000
66666666666666666666666666600000000006
66666666666666666666666666666600000006
66666666666666666666666666666666600060
6666666666666666666666666666666666666
```

← CENTER

MINI-LOOM SIZE
3" wide by 4" long (center opening)

41. ORCA JOY
JUMP LEFT

BEADS
size 11° seed beads

CODE	COLOR	COUNT
θ	grey trans luster	104
1	light sapphire trans luster	674
2	garnet trans	18
3	hyacinth (orange) trans	18
4	citrine (yellow) trans	18
5	emerald trans	18
6	cobalt (blue) trans	276
7	deep amethyst trans	15
8	black matte	187
9	white opal	91
0	crystal aurora borealis (AB)	98

THREAD

SIZE	COLOR	LENGTH
O	white	5 yards
B	white	6 yards

NEEDLES

#12 extra long

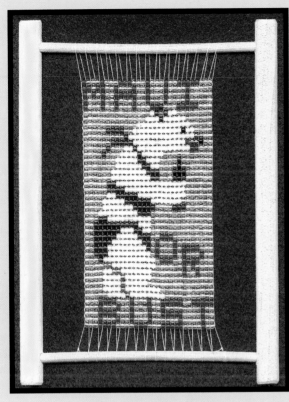

45. MAUI OR BUST

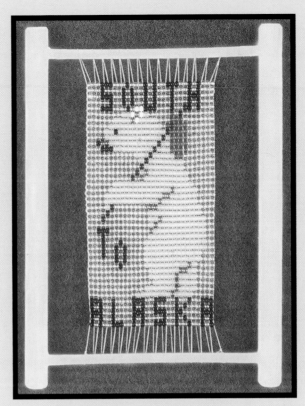

46. SOUTH TO ALASKA

47. CANDLELIGHT

48. CHRISTMAS TREE

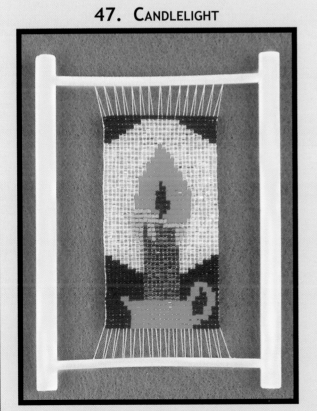

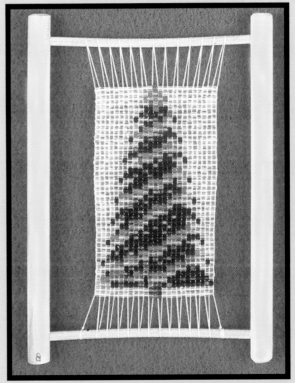

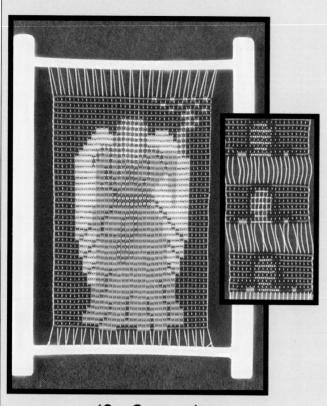

49. CRYSTAL ANGEL

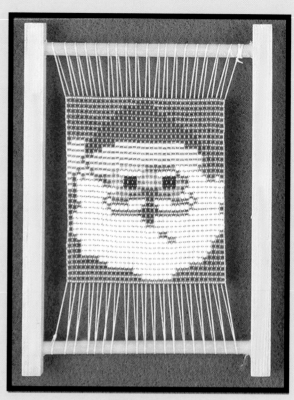
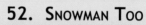

50. SANTA

51. SNOWMAN

52. SNOWMAN TOO

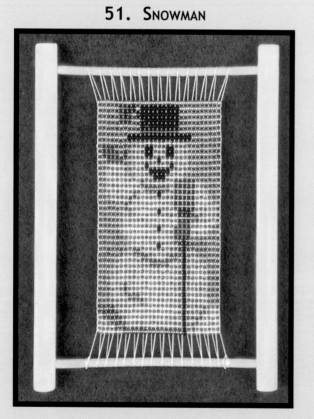

42. ORCA JOY
YES!!

```
23456711111111111111111111111111765432
34567111111111111111111111111111176543
45671111111111111111111111199811117654
56711111111111111111111111119999881111765
67111111111111111111111119999999881111176
71111111111111111111111119999999881111117
11111111111111111111119999999898111111111
11111111188888888889999999998981111111
11111111188888888888999999998981111111
11111118888888888889999999988881111111
11111118888888888889988898888811111111
11111118888888888818999888888881111111
11111111888888888818999888888881111111
11111111111111111118998888888881111111
11111111110111111189998888888881111111
11111110111111111189998888888881111111
11111111111110111189988888888881111111
11111111110111111189988888888881111111
11111111111111111189988888888888111111
11111111101111111189988888888888811111
11111101111111111189988888888888811111
11111111111101111899888888888811111111
11111110111111111899888888888811116611
66111111116611111899888888888111666666
66661111166666111899988888888066666666
66666666666666666699998888888060666666
66660666066666666699999998888006666666
66666666666666666689988999888806066666
66666666666666666688988899888066066666
66666666666666666689888899888060660666
66666666666666666689988898880066066666
66666666666666666689888898880066066666
00000000066666666668988898800066660666
00000000066666666660088800880066066666
00000066666666600000666000880000000666
66666000000000000066666000000000666666
66666000000000066666660000000000000666
66666666000006666666600000000000666666
66666666666666666666066660000000000066
66666666666666666666600000000000000000
66666666666666666666666666666666666666
```

MINI-LOOM SIZE
3" wide by 4" long (center opening)

CENTER

BEADS
size 11° seed beads

CODE	COLOR	COUNT
1	light sapphire trans luster	517
2	garnet trans	2
3	hyacinth (orange) trans	4
4	citrine (yellow) trans	6
5	emerald trans	8
6	cobalt (blue) trans	391
7	deep amethyst trans	12
8	black matte	300
9	white opal	118
0	crystal aurora borealis (AB)	159

THREAD

SIZE	COLOR	LENGTH
O	white	5 yards
B	white	6 yards

NEEDLES

#12 extra long

43. UNDER THE SEA

```
2222222222222222211111111111111112222222
2222222222211111111222222222222222222222
2222111111111122222222223322221111111111
1111111111122222221333333331111111112222
1111111222422222333333333331112222222222
1111222224422113333333333332222222222211
2222222224441113333333333333332222222111
2222211444411333333333333332222221111
1111114444111333333223333331111111122
1111114444222333333331133333311111111222
2222222444422233333331111333311111122222
2222111444434433333331111333222222211
1111144441333333333332222233322222111
1111444411333333333332222222222111111
1111444422333333333332222111111111222
2222444422333333333331111111111222222
2222244442233333333333311111122222222111
2222114111333333333331114222222222111
4111144411331333333311442222222111111
4411144411322333333224442211111111111
4442224222223333322444442111111111222
4442224222223333324444411111112222222
2442224111133331144444111112222222111
1144114111333334444444422222222222211111
2244424222333343333442222221111111111
1114414113331433333311111111111111222
1111141113334434444331111111122222222111
1111141133314444443311111222222211111
2222242233324444223322222222211111111
2222242234442222223322221111111112222
4111141144431111133111111111222222111
4411141144333333331111111222222222111
4441114411133333322222222222221111111
2442224222222222222222222211111122222
2442224111111111111111112222222222111
2244114111111111111122222222222211111
1144114111111112222222221111111111122
1111141111122222222211111111222222222
2222242222222221111111111111222222222
2222242222221111111122222222222222222
2222242222111111111111112222222222222
```

CENTER (marked at the row `4442224222223333322444442111111111222`)

MINI-LOOM SIZE
3" wide by 4" long (center opening)

BEADS
size 11° seed beads

CODE	COLOR	COUNT
1	light sapphire trans luster	540
2	kelly green trans luster	557
3	topaz trans	258
4	dark smoke topaz trans	162

THREAD

SIZE	COLOR	LENGTH
O	white	5 yards
B	white	6 yards

NEEDLES

#12 extra long

44. U.S.A.

```
11111111111111111111111111111111
11121111211111222221111222211111
11121111211111211111111121111211
11121111211111211111111121111211
11121111211111222211111121111211
11121111211111111121111222221111
11121111211111111121111211111211
11112222112112222211211211112121
11111111111111111111111111111111
11111111111111111111111111111111
11111111111111111111111111111111
1333333333333444444441111111111
1353535353533555555554444111111
1353535353534444444455554444441
1353535353533555555555544445555551
1353535353534444444455554444441
1353535353533555555555544445555551
1333333333333444444444455554444441
1555555555555555555555544445555551
1444444444444444444444455554444441
1555555555555555555555544445555551
1444444444444444444444455554444441
1555555555555555555555544445555551
1444444444444444444444455554444441
11111111111111111111111144445555551
11111111111111111111111111114444441
11111111111111111111111111111111
11111111111111111111111111111111
11111111111111111111111111111111
11112222211111222111111222221111
11112222221112222111122222211111
11111222222211222112222222111111
11111112222222222222222221111111
11111111222222222222222221111111
11111111122222222222222221111111
11111111112222222222221111111111
11111111111222222221111111111111
11111111111112222211111111111111
11111111111111222111111111111111
11111111111111222221111111111111
11111111111112222222111111111111
11111111111122222222111111111111
11111111111121212121211111111111
11111111111111111111111111111111
```

CENTER

BEADS
size 11° seed beads

CODE	COLOR	COUNT
1	light aqua trans luster	832
2	dark smoke topaz trans	211
3	cobalt (blue) trans	59
4	garnet trans	175
5	white pearl	175

THREAD

SIZE	COLOR	LENGTH
O	white	5 yards
B	white	6 yards

NEEDLES

#12 extra long

MINI-LOOM SIZE
3" wide by 4" long (center opening)

45. Maui Or Bust

```
2111211122211121112112222211 1
221221121112112112111121111 1
212121122222112111211112111 1
211121121112112112111121111 1
211121121112111223111222221 11
111111111111111738377111111 11
111111111111111777377777111 11
111111111111777777777777111 11
111113333117777777777477111 1
111111111137777777777777775 111
111111333337777777777255411
111113111773777777777722111
111131117777377777111111111 1
111111177777337771111611111 11
111111177777337771116111111 1
111111777777733311116661111 11
111111777777773311166611111 1
111113377777777777777711111 1
111113333777777777777711111 1
111117733333777777777711111 1
111177773333337777776111111   ———CENTER
111177777733333111166611111
111777777733311111111111111 1
111337777777771111111111111 1
113333333333777111111111111 11
113333337773377111111111111 1
113333377773331122211111111 1
113333777777331211121111111 1
113337777777731211121222211 1
113337777777771211121211211
111377777777771222112222111
111155777777777111112121111
111177557777777111112112111
111177757777771111111111111
111177757777711111111111111
111177757777777111111111111
111117775777777711111111111
111122221112111211222221122 222
111121112112111211211111111 211
111222211121112112222211111 211
111211121121112111111121111 211
111222211112221112222211111 211
```

MINI-LOOM SIZE
3" wide by 4" long (center opening)

BEADS
size 11° seed beads

CODE	COLOR	COUNT
1	crystal aurora borealis (AB)	653
2	garnet trans	132
3	deep amethyst trans	94
4	black opaque	2
5	grey trans	11
6	dark smoke topaz trans	12
7	white opal	313
8	citrine (yellow) trans	1

THREAD

SIZE	COLOR	LENGTH
O	white	5 yards
B	white	6 yards

NEEDLES

#12 extra long

46. SOUTH TO ALASKA

```
111222111211121211222211212111
111211112121121211112111212111
111222112121121211112111222111
111112112121121211112111212111
111222111213322211121117212111
111111118834381111161711111111
111111888843888811166611111111
111118888888888881676661111111
111188588888888887666611111111
111488888888888887866661111111
115448888888888887886666111111
111555888888888788866661111111
111111111188878888866111111111
111111111111878888888811111111
111111111111788888888811111111
111111111117848888888881111111
111111111171488888888881111111
111111888888888888888811111111
111118888888888888488888811111
111188888888888884488888811111
111188888888888848888888811111
111187111111144488888888811111
111171111111118888888888811111
111711111111118848888888881111
111111111111118488888888881111
112221111111114888888888881111
111211111111118888888888881111
111211121111188888888888881111
111211212111188888888888881111
111211212111188888888888881111
111111212111188888888888881111
111111121111188888888888481111
111111111111188888888448811111
111111111111188888848888811111
111111111111118888848888811111
111111111111188888848888811111
111111111118888888848888111111
222112111122211222112112 11222
212112111121211211112121 11212
222112111122211222112211 11222
212112111121211121121211 11212
212112221121211222112112 11212
```

MINI-LOOM SIZE
3" wide by 4" long (center opening)

CENTER

BEADS
size 11° seed beads

CODE	COLOR	COUNT
1	crystal aurora borealis (AB)	631
2	cobalt (blue) trans	127
3	white opaque	5
4	grey trans	24
5	black opaque	5
6	garnet trans	26
7	dark smoke topaz trans	15
8	white opal	385

THREAD

SIZE	COLOR	LENGTH
O	white	5 yards
B	white	6 yards

NEEDLES

#12 extra long

47. CANDLELIGHT

```
1111111111111111111111111111111
1111111111122222222211111111111
1111111112222222222222211111111
1111111222222222222222222111111
1111222222222222222222222221111
1122222222222222222222222222211
2222222222222223222222222222222
2222222222222233322222222222222
2222222222222233332222222222222
2222222222223343332222222222222
2222222222223334333222222222222
2222222222223344433322222222222
2222222222233444443332222222222
2222222222333444444332222222222
2222222222334441444333222222222
2222222222334441144433222222222
2222222223444111444433222222222
2222222223444111444332222222222
2222222223444111144433222222222
2222222223444151144433222222222
2222222266664451444333222222222
2222222666666654443333222222222
2222222666666666433332222222222
2222222666766677666662222222222
2222222666766777766662222222222
2222222666766777766622222222222
2222222266776777766222222222222
2222222226777777766222222222222
2222222226777777772222222222222
2222222227777777772222222222222
1122222227777777772222222211
1111222222777777772222221111
1111112222777777772222111111
1111111122777777772211111111
1111111111777777771111111111
1111111111777777771111111111
1111111111777777771111444111
1111111111777777771114414411
1111111111777777771114411441
1111111111777777771114411441
111144111177777777114411441
1111144444444444444441111441
1111114444444444444441114411
1111111444444444444441114411
1111111444444444444444444111
1111111444444444444444411111
1111111444444444444441111111
```

CENTER

MINI-LOOM SIZE
3" wide by 4" long (center opening)

BEADS
size 12° two-cut beads

CODE	COLOR	COUNT
1	cobalt (blue) trans	318
2	citrine (yellow) trans luster	567
3	china red opaque	69
4	red opaque	185
5	black opaque	3
6	turquoise opaque	54
7	emerald trans luster	138

THREAD

SIZE	COLOR	LENGTH
O	white	5 yards
B	white	6 yards

NEEDLES

#13
#15

84

48. CHRISTMAS TREE

```
11111111111141111111111111
11111111111145411111111111
11111111111454541111111111
11111111111145411111111111
11111111111224221111111111
11111111112322324111111111
11111111121133241211111111
11111111111224451111111111
11111111112445532111111111
11111111144553322211111111
11111112112322211121111111
11111111123222441111111111
11111111132224455511111111
11111112234455523221111111
11111121145523221121111111
11111111552232222211111111
11111112223232222441111111
11111122322322244555111111
11111211222444552112111111
11111112224555222231111111
11111112244523323224111111
11111444552322224455111111
11112115323222245511121111
11111115322224445223111111
11111222232455552222211111
11112322224532223223211111
11121123445222322222112111
11111224552232232224111111
11112445323222322234551111
11144552322222244452221111
11211522222224555231121111
11112232232444523222211111
11123223244555222232241111
11322244552322322224455111
12114455523223222445511211
11155523224222244552321111
11244422445444455222222211
14455544552555552223232221
55522322232566232222222232
11111111111166611111111111
11111111111166611111111111
```

CENTER ← (at row 20)

MINI-LOOM SIZE
3" wide by 4" long (center opening)

BEADS
size 11° two-cut beads

CODE	COLOR	COUNT
1	crystal aurora borealis (AB)	537
2	dark green transparent	243
3	light green transparent	60
4	garnet transparent	90
5	topaz transparent	87
6	dark smoke topaz trans	8

THREAD

SIZE	COLOR	LENGTH
O	white	5 yards
B	white	5 yards

NEEDLES

#12 extra long
#13

```
11111111111111111111111101101101011 01
11111111111111111111111111011101110111
11111111111111111111111111110111011101
11111111111111111111111111111111110011111
1111111111111111133333111111111014111
11111111111111133444331111111114441111
1111111112221134444431122211441111111
1111111112222233444443222222144111111
1111111112222223344444322222224411111 1
1111111122223333344433333222244111111
11111122223353334444355335554411 1111
11111222233535353544457355355522211111
111112222355535353754575355535522211111
1111122222553653575753555555522211111
1111122222553653557555355525522211111
11111222225536355757535552255222211111
11111222225365575557555222552221 1111
11111222225555675555575222225222 11111
1111122222555577777776222252221 1111
1111122222555577777777262225222 11111
111112222555565555755555526222222211111
1111122222555655557575555552622222211111
1111122225565555755755555552622221 1111
111112226556555575575555555226221 1111
11111226225655557557555555522262211111
1111126222655555757555555555222621 1111
111111222625555757555555555562221 11111
111111226255557575555555555526221 1111
1111112622555575575555555555222621 11111
11111112225555557555555555522211 11111
11111112265555555555555555556221111111
11111112625555655555555555552621111111
1111111122556555555555555555211111111
111111122556555555555555556555111111111
11111111155556555555555555565511 1111111
11111111155655555655555556555 11111111
11111111155555556555556555655111111111
111111111555556555655556555655111111 1111
11111111155555655556555565555511 1111
11111111555556555565555565556555111111
111111115555565555555555565555555111111
111111111115555111115551555111111111
```

49. CRYSTAL ANGEL

CENTER

MINI-LOOM SIZE
3" wide by 4" long (center opening)

Note: With the understanding that angels are for everyone, "Crystal Angel" has been designed with different skin tones and different hair colors. The <u>skin</u> tones are represented by <u>Code #4</u>, and the <u>hair</u> by <u>Code #3</u>. Before purchasing the beads for this project, choose one skin and one hair color.

BEADS
size 11° seed beads

CODE	COLOR	COUNT
1	dark aqua trans matte	662
2	white opal	224
3	black opaque	
	- OR - topaz trans luster	57
4	grey trans luster	
	- OR - light topaz	
	- OR - smoke topaz	
	- OR - pale pink	44
5	aqua AB matte	446
6	grey AB matte	58
7	gold supra (metallic)	48
0	crystal aurora borealis (AB)	15

THREAD

SIZE	COLOR	LENGTH
A	white	5 yards
B	white	6 yards

NEEDLES

#12 extra long

50. SANTA

```
00000000000000000000000000000000000000000
00000000000000001111000000000000000000000
00000000000001111111100000000000000000000
00000000000011111111111000000000000000000
00000000000111111111111111100000000000000
00000000011111111111111111111000000000000
00000001111111111111111111111110000000000
00000011111111111111111111111111110000000
03330111111333333333333333331111100000
33331111333333333333333333333333100000
33332233333333333333333333333333300000
33323333333333333333333333333333300000
33332333333334444442222222666330000000
33233233334466666444466662666660000000
32623332224444777444444777742266660060
32666666224447774444447774426666666
32666666666455555111155555266666666
02666666624455222211222255662666666
02666666262222666622666622226266666
00266666626666666622226666666266666660
22666666662222222211112222222666666660
26666666666666666662116666666666666666
26666666666666666662266666666666666666
26666666666666666666666666666666666666
26666666666666666666662266666666666660
02666666666666666666666226666666666600
00266666666666666666666666666666666000
00266666666666666666666666666666666000
00266666666666666666666666666666660000
000222266666666666666666666666600000
00000022666666666666666666600000000
000000000222222666666666600000000000
00000000000000002666666600000000000
00000000000000000000000000000000000000
```

CENTER

MINI-LOOM SIZE
3" wide by 4" long (center opening)

BEADS
size 11° seed beads

CODE	COLOR	COUNT
0	peridot trans luster	352
1	garnet transparent	131
2	grey transparent	103
3	crystal aurora borealis (AB)	130
4	pale pink	37
5	deep pink	14
6	white opaque	445
7	cobalt (blue) transparent	12

THREAD

SIZE	COLOR	LENGTH
O	white	5 yards
B	white	6 yards

NEEDLES

#12 extra long

51. Snowman

```
0000000000000000000000000000000
0000033220111111110000000000
0000032302111111110000000000
0000033300211111110000000000
0000000000121111110000000000
0000000000333333330000000000
0000000011111111111111110000000
0000000004444444444000000000
0333000004441144411444000000000
0333303044411444114440000000000
0033330044444414444440000000000
0044440044414444414444000000000
0044440044441111144440000000000
0044444004444111444400000000
0044444445444444466666400000
0044444444555555466666440000
0044444454444414446666644000
0004444544444444446666644400
0000045444444444446666644440
0000044544444414444777544440
0000044444444444446665544440
0000044444444444443334444440
0000044444444414443333444400
0000004444444444433334444000
0000000444444444455575000000
0000000044444441444457500000
0000004455444444445744000000
0000044444554444455474440000
0000444444455555444744440000
0004444444444444444744444000
0004444444444444444744444000
0004444444444444444744440000
0004445444444444444744444000
0004445444444444444744444000
0004445554444444444744444000
0004444445444444444744444000
5555444444444444444744445444
4555544444444444444744454444
4455544444444444444744544444
4444555444444444444745444444
4444445555555555555744444444
```

MINI-LOOM SIZE
3" wide by 4" long (center opening)

— CENTER

BEADS
size 11° seed beads

CODE	COLOR	COUNT
0	light aqua trans luster	386
1	black opaque	72
2	kelly green trans	6
3	garnet trans	39
4	crystal aurora borealis (AB)	568
5	grey trans	70
6	topaz trans	28
7	dark smoke topaz trans	20

THREAD

SIZE	COLOR	LENGTH
O	white	4 yards
B	white	5 yards

NEEDLES
#12 extra long

52. SNOWMAN TOO

```
1111111111111111111111111
1111111112222222133441111
1111111112222222314341111
1111111112222223114441111
1111111112222232111111111
1111111114444444111111111
1111112222222222222111111
1111111100000000011111111
1111111000220220001111444
1111111000002000001414444
1111111002000002001144441
1111111000222220001100001
1111111100000000011000001
1111155555000000000000001
1110555550002000060000001
1100555550000000006000001
1000555550000000000600011
0000777700020000060000011
0000655500000000000000111
0000644400000000000001111   ← CENTER
1000044440002000000011111
1100044440000000000111111
1111117600000000060111111
1111107000000666600011111
1111007000006600000001111
1110007000000000000000111
1100607000000000000000011
1100607000000000000000011
1106007000000000000000011
1100007000000000000060011
1100007000000000060600011
1100007000000000006000011
0060007000000000000000660
0006007000000000000006660
0000607000000000000066660
0000067000000000000666600
0000007666666666666666600
0000000006666666666660000
0000000000006666666600000
```

MINI-LOOM SIZE
3" wide by 4" long (center opening)

BEADS
size 11° two-cut beads

CODE	COLOR	COUNT
0	crystal aurora borealis (AB)	480
1	light amethyst trans	281
2	black opaque	54
3	kelly green transparent	6
4	garnet transparent	37
5	light topaz transparent	23
6	light sapphire trans	74
7	dark topaz transparent	20

THREAD

SIZE	COLOR	LENGTH
O	white	4 yards
B	white	5 yards

NEEDLES

#12 extra long
#13

NOTES:

B. Beading Grid Paper

The following pages include beading grid paper for size 10^0, 11^0, 12^0, 13^0 and 14^0 seed beads, as well as "square" beading grid paper for the Delica's, 11^0 two-cuts and 12^0 two-cuts. The grids are presented according to bead type and size, with the recommended maximum number of vertical and horizontal rows to fit the mini-frame loom opening of 3 inches by 4 inches (3" x 4"). **Please note** that the Delica beads and the 12^0 two-cut beads use the same size grid.

This section also includes full-size beading grid paper for both the seed beads and the "square" beads, for those projects not intended for the mini-frame loom. The ovals and the squares making up these grids are not exactly the size of the beads, but rather the best representation possible while still allowing the crafter to design and color. If desired, the grids can be photocopied and reduced.

RECOMMENDED MAXIMUM ROWS FOR MINI-LOOM 3" X 4"

BEAD SIZE	VERTICAL ROWS	HORIZONTAL ROWS
10^0	38	40
11^0	40	45
12^0	45	48
13^0	50	52
14^0	55	56
11^0 Two Cut	35	48
12^0 Two Cut	42	50
Delica	42	50

The above chart is for guideline purposes only. As stated previously, bead sizes and shapes vary even within a given size range.

"Vertical Rows" refers to the bead count left to right. Consider the top row of the pattern. Each bead in this top row is representative of one vertical row consisting of all the beads directly beneath it.

"Horizontal Rows" refers to the bead count top to bottom. Consider the left edge of the pattern. Each bead in this edge row is the representative of one horizontal row consisting of all the beads directly to the right of it. The "top" and "bottom" of the pattern refer to its position on the mini-frame loom. The warp thread ties onto the bottom horizontal stick. The warp thread continues up and over the top horizontal stick and then back under the bottom one. Even when the completed picture will be turned $90°$ for displaying purposes, as with the Golden Eagle pattern, the "top" and "bottom" designations remain the same.

Beading Grid Paper
Recommended Maximum Rows For Mini-Loom 3" x 4"

Size 10⁰ Seed Beads

Size 13⁰ Seed Beads

BEADING GRID PAPER
RECOMMENDED MAXIMUM ROWS FOR MINI-LOOM 3" x 4"

Size 11⁰ Seed Beads

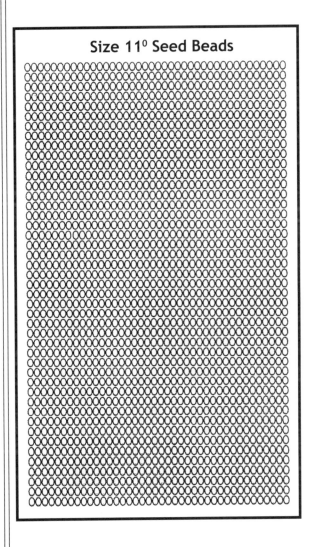

Size 12⁰ Seed Beads

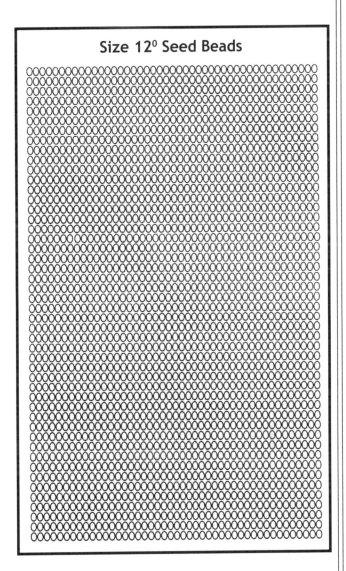

BEADING GRID PAPER
RECOMMENDED MAXIMUM ROWS FOR MINI-LOOM 3" x 4"

Size 14⁰ Seed Beads

BEADING GRID PAPER
RECOMMENDED MAXIMUM ROWS FOR MINI-LOOM 3" x 4"

Size 11⁰ 2-Cut Beads

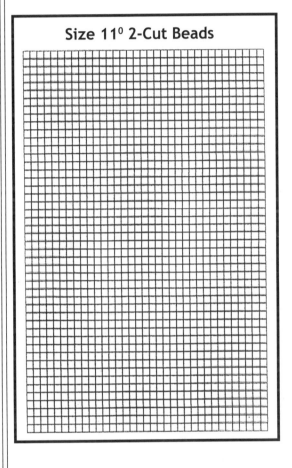

Size 12⁰ 2-Cut Beads and Delica Beads

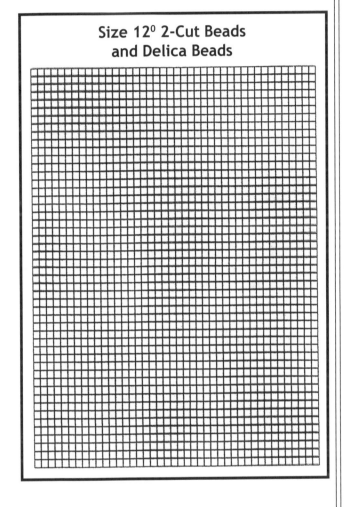

BEADING GRID PAPER FOR SEED BEADS

NOTES:

C: Tips

ESTIMATED BEADS PER HANK

Czech Seed Beads	Japanese Seed Beads	Czech 2-Cut Beads
(12 loops per hank)	(sold in tubes - by the gram)	(12 loops per hank)
10° 3100 beads	11° 100 beads per gram	11° 3580 beads
11° 4000 beads	14° 275 beads per gram	12° 4200 beads
12° 4500 beads		
13° 5000 beads	**French Seed Beads**	**Japanese Delica Beads**
14° 5580 beads	12° 130 beads per gram	215 beads per gram
(10 loops per hank)	13° 150 beads per gram	
13° Charlottes	14° 275 beads per gram	**Japanese 15° Hex Beads**
(true cuts) 2250		295 beads per gram

Bead packaging varies depending on manufacturer as well as retail sales techniques. These numbers are averages only, and are not be to construed as absolutes.

CONVERSIONS AND COMPARING PRICES

Some retail stores package and sell beads by the gram (generally a 20 gram bag). Other stores package and sell beads by the ounce. This makes it difficult to compare prices. The following conversions should be helpful in sorting out pricing.

1 Kilo	1/2 Kilo	
1000 grams	500 grams	1 ounce = 28.35 grams
2.2 pounds	1.1 pounds	1 gram = .035 ounces
35.27 ounces	17.5 ounces	

Consider the following: two stores carry the same size 14° Japanese opaque white seed beads. One store sells these beads by the 20 gram package while the other store sells them by the ounce.

STORE #1: $2.25 for 20 grams

STORE #2: $4.25 for 1 ounce

if "?" stands for price per gram, then
20 grams x "?" = 2.25
2.25 divided by 20 = "?"
2.25 divided by 20 = .1125 per gram

1 ounce = 28.35 grams
if "?" stands for price per gram, then
28.35 grams x"?" = 4.25
4.25 divided by 28.35 = "?"
4.25 divided by 28.35 = .1499 per gram

-OR-

STORE #1: $2.25 for 20 grams   **STORE #2:** <u>$4.25</u> per ounce

    20 x .035 = .7 ounces
    if "?" stands for price per ounce, then
    .7 x ? = 2.25
    2.25 divided by .7 ="?"
    2.25 divided by .7 = $3.21 per ounce

By the gram or by the ounce, store #2 is charging more for the same beads. It is difficult to compare beads sold by the hank versus beads sold in bulk, but it can be done by calculating the actual bead count. This is much harder than it sounds, because the actual bead count varies. Also consider that economic factors come into play. At the time of this writing, the beads from the Czech Republic are less expensive than the beads from Japan.

ESTIMATE OF BEADS PER SQUARE INCH OF LOOMWORK

Seed Beads		Two-Cut Beads	
10°	130	11°	182
11°	187	12°	255
12°	228	**Japanese Delica Beads**	
13°	273	255	
14°	322	**Japanese 15° Hex Beads**	
		361	

The "per inch" estimates vary depending on bead selection. Whether purchasing beads by the hank or the gram, from the Czech Republic, Japan or France, etc., there will be size variations. A piece loomed with the smallest of any given size, <u>will be smaller</u> than a piece worked with the largest beads of the same lot.

LOOMING AND BEADING TIPS

♦ There are times when keeping the tension and tying a square knot is difficult (i.e. when tying off the warp thread). If this occurs, the "surgeon's knot" can come in handy (see Diagram 8.1). Wrap the thread 3 or 4 times around the horizontal stick. Use a "surgeon's knot" first to prevent slipping, and then finish with a simple overhand knot. (This combination can be substituted for the square knot.) By passing through the loop 2-3 times before pulling taut, the thread will help to hold itself. It will take a little practice, but can be very useful. This also works for tying off the spreader string.

♦ Warp tie-on and tie-off knots <u>must</u> be located on the inside of the working area. Refer to Diagrams 4.10 and 4.11.

♦ For the last rows (top and bottom) pass through the row two additional times to strengthen the edge before working down (from top) or up (from bottom), exiting between two beads, and trimming the thread ends.

♦ Avoid using standard graph paper (little squares) for charting designs using seed beads.

- Thread Heaven™ thread conditioner can be used to protect weft threads in place of bee's wax.
- To facilitate threading, hold the needle eye in front of a white background.
- Nymo thread can be flattened by biting down on the end. The flattened end passes more readily through the needle eye than a rounded end.
- For some beaders, it is easier to thread the needle after waxing it.
- When using wax, check the needle eye for buildup.
- Move the needle up the thread frequently to prevent fraying.

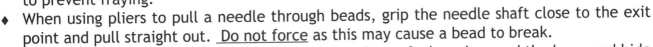

8.1 Tying a Surgeon's Knot

- When using pliers to pull a needle through beads, grip the needle shaft close to the exit point and pull straight out. <u>Do not force</u> as this may cause a bead to break.
- When not working on a piece, it is best to wrap the weft thread around the loom and hide the needle in a row of beads.
- For the energetic: consider brick stitch or peyote stitch on the dowel loom verticals (sides).
- A high-speed rotary tool (hand held) is helpful when small holes are needed to "build" sculptures.
- When working with glue, protect the table top with waxed paper.
- Keep glue to a minimum when assembling looms. Always remove excess glue before it dries.
- After sanding, wipe wood free of dust before applying paint or stain.
- Glue will hold better if all bark is scraped from areas to be glued.
- Using spreader strings top <u>and</u> bottom can be helpful when working on a loom with a longer opening, such as would be used for barrettes.
- Place a heavy, flat object (such as a book) on top of the stick or all-dowel loom to apply pressure and hold all in place while the glue is drying.
- Use waxed paper between the loom and the book to prevent damage to the book cover.
- When constructing a stick loom, try using slightly thicker sticks for the two vertical (side) pieces.
- Loomed pieces which will later be attached to leather or fabric (other than white in color) should be done with opaque style beads. The transparent beads allow background color to show through, thus muting the color of the beads.
- The plastic lid from a coffee or shortening can works well as a "shape holder" for barrettes.

Song Dog Suncatcher or Hanging Decoration

D. BIBLIOGRAPHY

Goodhue, Horace
Indian Bead-Weaving Patterns
Bead-Craft -1984

Hunt, W. Ben
Burshears, J.F. "Buck"
American Indian Beadwork
Collier Macmillan Publishing Company - 1971

Schneider, Richard C.
Crafts of the North American Indians
A Craftsman's Manual
R. Schneider Publishers - 1972

Smith, Monte
The Technique of North American Indian Beadwork
Eagle's View Publishing Company - 1983

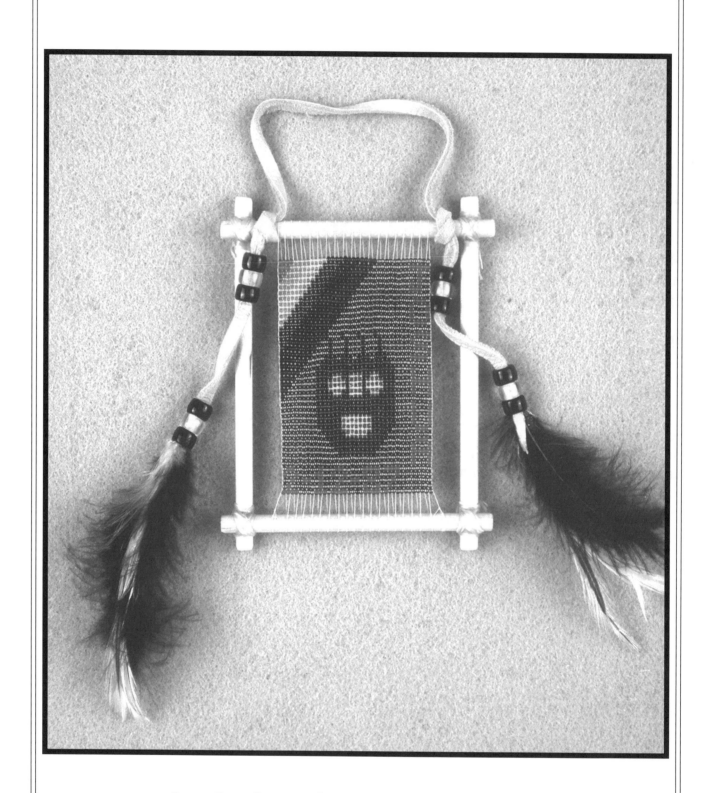

Bear Paw Suncatcher or Hanging Decoration

ABOUT THE AUTHOR

The author and two of her grandchildren

Mary Thompson was born in Milwaukee, Wisconsin and spent the first ten years of her childhood in that state. Since then she has lived primarily in California, with a short stint in Las Vegas. Mary currently resides in Virginia City, NV, in a log cabin which she and her husband built. She is married and has two daughters and four grandsons.

Mary tried her hand at several different hobbies before she walked into an Indian bead store in 1972 and experienced "a feeling of coming home". She bought a little roller loom, some beads, and went to work. It has been a love affair ever since and beadwork has opened many doors into new worlds for her. Mary started selling her work in 1985 and attracted the attention of Grandpa Semu Huaute, who eventually adopted her ceremonially as a Chumash and gave her his name to use. Diagnosed and treated for breast cancer in 1989, Mary considers herself a cancer survivor, rather than a victim. During her treatment and recovery, beadwork kept her going and lifted her spirits when needed.

Mary began teaching beadcraft in 1990 and became head teacher and class coordinator for a program in California. In 1991 she developed the mini-frame loom and then, kits using the mini-frame loom. Her bead work has won many prizes in the category of professional crafts and her loomwork sculptures have also won in the Fine Arts and Sculpture categories. She says that each finished piece is a song and that she teaches and writes to keep the craft alive and to introduce people of all age groups to the fun of loom beading.

BEADED TREASURE PURSES
Tubular Brick Stitch Designs
By
DEON DeLANGE

Let Deon, the Master of Brick Stitch, teach you an entirely new and easy way to make these very popular small beaded purses which are usually worn as necklaces. Deon's designs are one of her hallmarks and the ones in this book make incredibly beautiful purses using either delica beads or size 11 seed beads. The book introduces Tubular Brick Stitch techniques, which allow the beader to start every row at the edge of the pattern graph. This method is much easier to use than the more commonly taught techniques where the row starting points spiral around the beadwork. The book is fully illustrated with easy-to-follow instructions and lots of photographs. Each design is graphed by computer, making the patterns easy to read and follow. Included are many ideas for trimming the edges of a purse, as well as a variety of necklace strap suggestions. The exciting, new Freeform beading stitch is also introduced.

B00/42-$10.95

HEMP MASTERS:
Ancient Hippie Secrets for Knotting
Hip Hemp Jewelry

By MAX LUNGER

Learn to create with hemp. With the basic techniques taught in this book you can make Bracelets, Anklets, Necklaces, Chokers, Car Mirror Charms, Key Chains, Wall Tapestries, Plant Hangars, Speaker Hangers, Hackysacks and much more. Making hemp jewelry is the latest craze and it is easy to learn. The various knots needed are explained and fully illustrated. Included are details on incorporating beads within the knotting. After explaining how to begin a piece and providing useful tips on avoiding common problems, patterns for a variety of pieces are provided. This book is chock full of photographs (including a full color section) and has lots of illustrations. Written for both beginning and seasoned crafters, this volume will excite any person wishing to learn more about hemp knotting - Don't miss out on this exciting craft technique.

B00/31 - $13.95

BEADS AND BEADWORK OF THE AMERICAN INDIANS

By WILLIAM C. ORCHARD

The Eagle's View edition of this classic 1929 reference book has been reformatted for easier reading, but the text, plates and illustrations remain as in the 1975 edition. This, and Orchard's book on porcupine quill decoration, form the foundation for almost every text on Indian arts and crafts that has been written since their publication and they remain superior to most. The author dicusses the design motifs of finished beadwork and the role of early Europeans, whose colorful trade beads (shown in beautiful color plates) had such a tremendous impact. All of the basic techniques of beadwork are explored and illustrated. There are 16 color plates, 26 B&W plates and 136 figures which include drawings and photographs. Don't miss out on this reprint of a classic Native American reference book that will be invaluable to anyone with an interest in beads, American Indian culture or creating their own beadwork.

B00/08 - $16.95

A TREASURY OF BEADED JEWELRY:
Bead Stringing Patterns for All Ages

By MARY ELLEN HARTE

Dazzled by the beautiful beadwork of native peoples near and far? This culturally rich mix of sead bead patterns will satisfy the young beginner, the advanced crafter and the holiday giftmaker. Mel's new book makes learning to create beautiful necklaces, chokers, bracelets, belts, pouches and headbands a snap. From simple Y necklaces to elaborate Romanian collars and original designs by the author, each pattern is graphically diagrammed for easy use and is also accompanied by simple and clear written instructions. These are stringing patterns and require no elaborate stitching techniques. Explore this wonderful, diverse collection of seed bead patterns from around the world and collect a double bonus: The projects result in lovely, fashionable pieces which you and your friends will be proud to wear on any occasion. Six pages of color photographs add to the beauty of this 42 page book. A great new release you won't want to miss!

B00/44 - $8.95

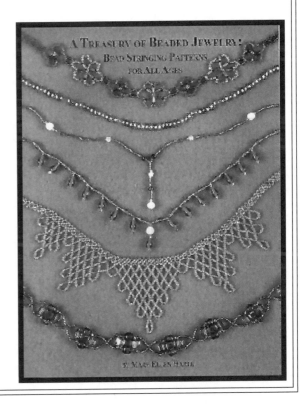

BEADED IMAGES:
Intricate Beaded Jewelry Using Brick Stitch
By BARBARA ELBE

Break out of the traditional Brick Stitch Earring mold! This book features new ideas and techniques designed to do just that. Barbara Elbe has produced a new series of designs which feature smaller beads (14/° seed beads, Hex beads, and Delica beads) and go beyond the conventional shapes usually seen in beaded earrings. Her designs are more detailed for their size, lighter in weight, and very original in appearance. This fully illustrated, how-to book contains complete instructions and 33 brand new patterns, including a chapter of nine Christmas Earrings and Pins. Each design is coded for level of difficulty. Once the new techniques are learned, readers can incorporate them into shapes and images of their own design. Included are Sculptured or Shaped Earrings which are created by increasing and decreasing the number of beads in each row to achieve different outlines. The book consists of 80 pages with 54 illustrations, 4 color plates and one black and white photo. An outstanding book for those seeking to stretch their creative legs!!

B00/35 - $9.95

CRAFT CORD CORRAL:
Bead Stringing Projects for Everyone
By JANICE S. ACKERMAN

This exciting book breaks new ground with fresh and innovative bead stringing projects that use pony beads, craft cord, and a variety of other large-hole beads. Embellished with conchos, feathers and other finery they bring an entirely new look to jewelry and home decorative items and it's easy! Contains complete step-by-step directions and is well illustrated with clear concise drawings. Projects include: Thunderbird Choker, Flower Necklace & Earring Set, Dream Catcher Necklace, Eye Glass Chain, Butterfly Waist Cincher, Concho Belt & Earring Set, Southwest Key Chain, a 5 inch Dream Catcher, and many more! Substitutions in the materials used result in entirely different looks for a given project and this practice is encouraged. Examples of projects using plastic facetted beads, colored leather thong, different colors of pony beads and different concho shapes from those originally suggested are pictured and briefly explained. Everyone will have fun making these projects and get results of which they can be proud.

B00/30 - $8.95

EAGLE'S VIEW BEST SELLERS

❏	Eagle's View Publishing Catalog of Books	B00/99	$4.00
❏	TheTechnique of Porcupine Quill Decoration by Orchard	B00/01	$9.95
❏	The Technique of North American Indian Beadwork by Smith	B00/02	$13.95
❏	Techniques of Beading Earrings by Deon DeLange	B00/03	$9.95
❏	More Techniques of Beading Earrings by Deon DeLange	B00/04	$9.95
❏	Art of Simulating Eagle Feathers by Bob Gutierres	B00/43	$9.95
❏	Crow Indian Beadwork by Wildschut and Ewers	B00/06	$10.95
❏	New Adventures in Beading Earrings by Laura Reid	B00/07	$9.95
❏	Voices of Native America by Douglas Spotted Eagle	B00/29	$17.95
❏	Traditional Indian Crafts by Monte Smith	B00/10	$9.95
❏	Traditional Indian Bead & Leather Crafts/ Smith/VanSickle	B00/11	$9.95
❏	Indian Clothing of the Great Lakes: 1740-1840/Hartman	B00/12	$14.95
❏	A Treasury of Beaded Jewelry: Bead Stringing Patterns by Mel Harte	B00/44	$8.95
❏	Adventures in Creating Earrings by Laura Reid	B00/14	$9.95
❏	Circle of Power by William Higbie	B00/15	$8.95
❏	Hemp Masters: Hip Hemp Jewelry by Max Lunger	B00/31	$13.95
❏	A Quillwork Companion by Jean Heinbuch	B00/17	$12.95
❏	Making Indian Bows & Arrows...The Old Way/Doug Spotted Eagle	B00/18	$12.95
❏	Making Arrows...The Old Way by Doug Spotted Eagle	B00/19	$4.50
❏	Hair of the Bear: Campfire Yarns & Stories by Eric Bye	B00/20	$9.95
❏	How To Tan Skins The Indian Way by Evard Gibby	B00/21	$4.95
❏	A Beadwork Companion by Jean Heinbuch	B00/22	$12.95
❏	Beads and Cabochons by Patricia Lyman	B00/23	$10.95
❏	Earring Designs by Sig: Book I by Sigrid Wynne-Evans	B00/24	$10.95
❏	Creative Crafts by Marj by Marj Schneider	B00/25	$9.95
❏	How To Bead Earrings by Lori Berry	B00/26	$10.95
❏	Delightful Beaded Earring Designs by Jan Radford	B00/27	$9.95
❏	Earring Designs by Sig: Book II by Sigrid Wynne-Evans	B00/28	$10.95
❏	Craft Cord Corral by Janice S. Ackerman	B00/30	$8.95
❏	Classic Earring Designs by Nola May	B00/32	$9.95
❏	Traditional Clothing of the Native Americans by Evard Gibby	B00/05	$17.95
❏	Plains Indian & Mountain Man Arts and Crafts by C. Overstreet	B00/34	$13.95
❏	Beaded Images: Intricate Beaded Jewelry by Barbara Elbe	B00/35	$10.95
❏	Earring Designs by Sig-Book III: Celebrations by S. Wynne-Evans	B00/36	$10.95
❏	Techniques of Fashion Earrings by Deon DeLange	B00/37	$9.95
❏	Beaded Images II: Intricate Beaded Jewelry by Barbara Elbe	B00/38	$9.95
❏	Picture Beaded Earrings for Beginners by Starr Steil	B00/39	$9.95
❏	Plains Indian & Mountain Man Arts and Crafts II by C. Overstreet	B00/40	$12.95
❏	Simple Lace and Other Beaded Jewelry Patterns by Mel Harte	B00/41	$6.95
❏	Beaded Treasure Purses by Deon DeLange	B00/42	$10.95

EAGLE'S VIEW PUBLISHING READERS SERVICE, DEPT BOMH-801
6756 North Fork Road - Liberty, Utah 84310

Please send me the above title(s). I am enclosing $_____ (Please add $5.50 per order to cover shipping and handling.) Send check or money order - no cash or C.O.D.s please.

Ms./Mrs./Mr. ————————————————————————————————————

Address ——————————————————————————————————————

City/State/Zip Code————————————————————————————————
Prices and availability subject to change without notice. Allow 2 to 3 weeks for delivery.

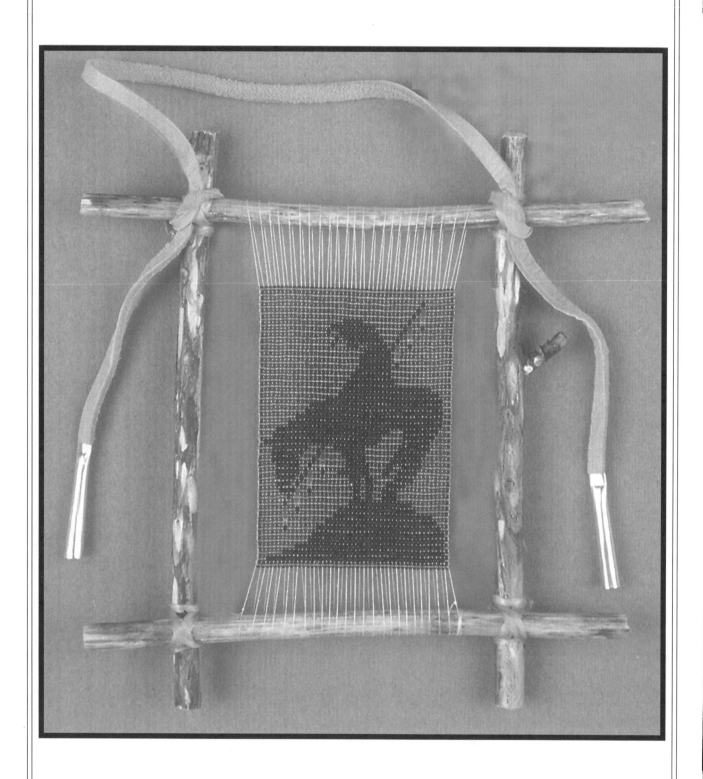

End of Trail Suncatcher or Hanging Decoration